Polarities in the Evolution of Mankind

West and East
Materialism and Mysticism
Knowledge and Belief

RUDOLF STEINER

Eleven lectures given to members of the Anthroposophical Society
in Stuttgart
5 March to 22 November 1920

Rudolf Steiner Press London
Anthroposophic Press New York.

Based on shorthand reports not revised by the lecturer.
German edition edited by Robert Friedenthal and Paul G. Bellmann,
Rudolf Steiner Nachlassverwaltung.

German title: Gegensätze in der Menschheitsentwickelung

1st German edition Dornach 1967
2nd German edition Dornach 1986
1st English Edition 1987

ISBN paper 0 85440 5461
RSP cloth 0 85440 2055
A P paper 0 88010 5569
cloth 0 88010 2063

Gesamtausgabe (Collected Works) No. 197
Typeset by Grassroots, London
Cover design by Studio Belacane
Printed in Great Britain by Whitstable Litho, Kent

CONTENTS

Stuttgart 5 March 1920 The development of conscious awareness; luciferic and ahrimanic spirits. Early humanity thinking in images and dependent on higher spirits. Gradual separation from those spirits; intellectual thinking developing to train humans in freedom. Ahriman's aims and purposes. Opposition in Norway.   1

Stuttgart 7 March 1920 Different potentials of Asians and Europeans. Need to understand Christ in a new way. Development of the intellect from beginning of post-Atlantean period. Intelligence developed in soul and spirit in the Orient and at the physical level in Europe. East accepted Christianity into the soul in a way incomprehensible to modern European scientists. The rational Western mind was bound to the physical body and could not understand the Mystery of Golgotha. Goetheanism. Theosophy of the Theosophical Society as pre-Christian wisdom. Initiation the precondition for social thinking.   15

Stuttgart 9 March 1920 Changing awareness in political life. Empires evolving in three stages on earth. Stage 1: Imperialism of partly prehistoric times; earthly and hierarchic order one. Present-day example—pastoral from a bishop. Stage 2: Ruler by the grace of God. Example: Holy Roman Empire. Stage 3: Substance lost from words and symbols. Phrase and convention instead. Need for new social impulses.   27

Stuttgart 13 June Powers of decline in present-day civilization. Secret societies, Jesuitism and Leninism: three initiation streams in the present day. Religious confessions opposing   41 spiritual science. Their denial of pre-existence and dogma of eternal hell. Professor Traub's smear campaign. Opposition from Roman Catholic Press in Switzerland.

Stuttgart 24 June 1920 Decline of human civilization as a consequence of materialism. Material world can only be truly understood in the spirit. Materialistic view of the human heart as a pump. Head as the fruit of previous life on earth. Materialistic view of history. Economic life as head organ of the social organism, the sphere of rights as its rhythmical organ and cultural life as its metabolic organ. Threefold social order, Waldorf School, Kommender Tag. The destructive quality of untruthfulness. Spiritual science and and practical life.   55

Stuttgart 25 July 1920 Materialism and mysticism. True perceptiveness as a deed of the human soul. Disguised materialism in theosophy and spiritism. Materialism of modern science. Mysticism gives experience of physical matter by revealing material processes within the human organism. Mysticism as a disease. Need for transition from experience in space to one in time. Nature of force of gravity. Inner experience of force of gravity. Ahriman, Lucifer, Christ.   72

Stuttgart 30 July 1920 Materialism and mysticism on the wrong road. Active perceptiveness in Anthroposophy. Looking for nature of matter in the phenomena of the outside world leads to feeblemindedness; looking for the spirit by practising inner mysticism leads to childishness. Politics an illusion: Conservative element ahrimanic, liberal element luciferic. Fight of Jesuits against Anthroposophy. Rightness of materialism in its own sphere.   87

Stuttgart 21 September 1920 Distinction between knowledge and belief. Ancient wisdom had to fade to make freedom possible. As modern science evolved, knowledge   102 reduced to mere belief. Jesuitism. Rome as the source spring of materialism. No longer inner experience connecting with words. Need to speak of human existence before birth. The threefold social order and its opponents.

Stuttgart 8 November 1920 East, Middle and West. The threefold social order. Sleeping and waking. The threefold nature of the human being. In the East, life before birth was experienced in the spirit. This spirit has grown decadent. In the Middle, culture of material world and spirit, eminence given to thinking (Hegel). West: material culture, yet also preparation for future Imaginations; incipient awareness of principles that go beyond death. In the East: instinctive wisdom; in the Middle; dialectics, intellectual life; in the West: materialism, spirit of economics. East: end (example of Tolstoy); West: beginning (example of Keely). Mission of the Middle for the present. 117

Stuttgart 14 November 1920 Transition from luciferic to ahrimanic age and the Christ event to come. Technology; human beings and machines. Ahrimanic demons active in the present, luciferic elemental spirits in the past. Appearance of the etheric Christ in the present time. Ahrimanization of the world. Increasing stress in human souls. Need to prepare for the Christ event. 135

Stuttgart 22 November 1920 The impersonal attitude of modern science. The Christ spirit which has to enter into science. The threefold social order as 20th century Goetheanism. Spirit-self, life-spirit and spirit-man cannot evolve through forces provided by the earth but only through the Christ. Schiller's letters on aesthetic education and Goethe's Tale. The mystery play *The Portal of Initiation* as a metamorphosis of the creative potential in Goethe's Tale. Golden, Silver and Brazen Kings representing the three aspects of the social organism. 154

Notes 173
Index of names 184

Stuttgart, 5 March 1920

The challenges presented by our age really have to be faced by every individual human being today. I have made it quite clear on a number of occasions that to understand the way individuals need to face those challenges we must be aware of how human evolution progresses all over the globe. The whole course of human evolution can only be clearly understood if we gain more profound insight into the powers that intervene in the course of earth evolution as a whole and also in human lives.

I have used a number of different approaches to show that as human beings we are part of an ongoing evolution that may be said to be taking its normal course. Spiritual science enables us to follow its progress over extended periods of time. I have also pointed out that there are certain powers that have different goals for mankind than the powers who desire to guide humankind in the normal course of evolution, a course during which the earth repeatedly comes to physical manifestation. Some of those powers we would call luciferic, others ahrimanic. I have spoken of this a number of times. It is necessary to take a very serious view of these things today, but our hearts and minds cannot really achieve this serious mood unless we pay proper attention to the way these luciferic and ahrimanic powers intervene directly in human lives.

As you know, a new era in human evolution started during the 15th century, very different from anything that went before. Thinking of this you will want to be aware of the many ways in which life is different in the present age, which had its beginning in the 15th century, if we compare it to the preceding age. We may say that one particular feature of the present age is that intellectual thinking has developed since the middle of the 15th century. Humankind has to undergo a major process of education in the course of Earth evolution. Part of it is this training of the intellect. Human beings had to find out, as it were, how human life can be lived when the emphasis is on intellectual thinking. They could never have been raised to be truly free individuals if the intellectual principle had not become part of them. We have no clear idea today of the extent to which people differed from us before the middle of the 15th century, particularly in this respect. We tend to take the things we are given for granted, without giving them much thought. We are now generally dealing with the peoples of civilized countries who are inclined to think with the intellect, and we have come to believe that people have always been thinking like this. That is not the case, however, Before the middle of the 15th century people were thinking in a different way. They simply did not think in the abstract terms in which we think today. Their thinking was very much more vivid and concrete, immediately bound up with the objects of the world around them. They were much more bound up with the feelings and will impulses that can be experienced in the human soul. We are living very much in our thoughts, though we are not sufficiently aware of this. We are not even aware of the source from which this way of thinking, the intellectual approach which we take so much for granted, has evolved. We shall have to go a long way back in human evolution to get a real understanding of the origins of this way of thinking, this intellectualism. Another question we must ask ourselves is whether anything still remains of the human activity out of which our thinking has evolved.

You know that older evolutionary forces persist into later ages and continue to be present side by side with those that are normal to the age in question. This also applies to our thinking. Reminders, echoes of thinking, of an activity similar to our thinking are experienced in our dreams, when a whole world of images emerges from our night time sleep. Experience teaches us to distinguish between the world of thoughts we evolve between waking up and going to sleep and the world of dream images which we experience in an entirely passive way. If we go back to earlier times in human evolution we find that the further back we go the more does the life of the soul during waking hours come to resemble the mental activity we know in our dreams today. Present-day thinking is the fruit of later stages of evolution. During earlier stages along this path the human soul developed activities more akin to dreaming. If we follow this dreamlike activity of the human soul a long way back we find ourselves going beyond

Earth evolution as we know it. We come to a time when the earth had taken a physical form in the cosmos that preceded the present one. We have got used to calling it the Old Moon evolution. Human beings were part of this as well, but in an entirely different form. During that Moon evolution, i.e. the time when the earth materialized in a form that preceded the present one, the human being, the true ancestor of modern man, was still completely etheric. His soul became active in a way that was definitely dreamlike, consisting of dream images. The peculiar thing about this was that it related to the outer world in a way that is quite different from the soul activity we know as thinking. I would say that when our soul is active in thought we find ourselves rather isolated within the world. The world is outside us, it has its own processes. We reflect on those processes in our minds, but just when we think we are reflecting most profoundly on those external processes we actually feel ourselves entirely outside them. Indeed we often feel that we are best able to think about those external processes if we keep ourselves well isolated from them, withdrawing into ourselves. The human ancestor who was dreamy in his thinking, if I may put it like this, did not have that feeling. Developing in his way in his dreams what we develop in our way when we are thinking, he knew himself to be intimately bound up in everything he experienced with what went on in the world. We see the clouds, we think about them, but we do not feel that the powers alive in the clouds are also alive in our thinking. Our human ancestor did have the feeling that the powers alive in a cloud were also alive in his thinking. This ancestor said—and I must translate what he said into our language, for his language was a silent one compared to ours: The powers that are alive and active in the cloud out there produce images in my mind. He saw himself no more isolated from the great universe in which the cloud revealed its essential nature than my little finger is able to think itself isolated from the rest of me. If I were to cut it off it would wither; it would no longer be my finger. The human ancestor felt that he could not exist apart from the universe that belonged to him. My little finger might well say: The blood which pulses through the whole of the body also pulses within me; the whole of my organic life is governed by the same laws as the organic life of the rest of the body. The human ancestor said: I am part of the universe; the power that pulses within me as I evolve images is the same as the power that is alive and active in the forming of clouds. That is how the human ancestor felt himself to be closely related, intimately bound up, with the whole world.

We need to feel isolated from everything that goes on outside us in our thinking, as though the umbilical cord has been cut and we are separate from the essential origins and causes of the existing world. In ordinary life we are not aware of the pulses beating throughout the universe. Our thinking has grown abstract. Our thinking tells us nothing, as it were, of what is alive and active within it. This provides the actual potential for the freedom of human beings, a freedom where we do not feel that something is thinking in us but that we ourselves do the thinking.

The human ancestor was unable to form ideas independently of the universe as a whole. The human ancestor felt himself to be bound up with the existing world; he knew that this existing world contained more than just abstract forces of nature. He knew that power was also wielded by entities that differed from human beings, entities that did not have a physical body such as the human body, though human beings might feel that they had citizenry of the universe in common with them. The ancestor was not aware of 'forces of nature'; he felt himself to be in communion with nature spirits. Today we may say that everything that happens in nature follows the laws of nature, and we are part of that nature. For the human ancestor who lived in a far distant past it was natural to say that everything that happened in nature outside himself happened out of will impulses of the spirits of nature. We say the earth attracts the bodies that are on it due to gravity, and according to the law of gravity the gravitational pull decreases at a rate that is proportional to the square of the distance between the two objects. We call this a special case of a law of nature. When we speak of nature we base ourselves on such abstract notions. The human ancestor knew that an essential spiritual element was present in the phenomenon we have made into an abstract gravitational force.

Certain spiritual powers who may be said to be involved in human evolution thus developed a relationship to human beings. This would normally cease the moment Earth evolution proper began for the human being. At that point human beings would be released from the tutelage of those spiritual powers, powers they had felt to be flowing and floating into them during the Old Moon stage. So we must ask ourselves what it was that made human beings grow independent of the guidance of spirits with whom they had felt at one, however dimly. It happened when the mineral kingdom became part of human nature. In those far distant times of which I have just spoken, human beings did not yet have the mineral kingdom within them. Their organization would not have been perceptible to our present-day sense organs, for it did not yet include mineral elements.

To grasp this without getting caught up in preconceived notions we need to consider what it truly means when an organism includes the mineral kingdom. People tend to be superficial in their thinking about such things. We look at a mineral, a stone, and quite rightly consider it to be the way it presents itself to our observation. Then, however, we look at a plant in exactly the same way we look at a stone. In reality it is not the actual plant we see. A plant is really something entirely beyond sensory perception. Consider a system of forces that in a sense has the qualities of an image. Its relationship to the mineral kingdom is that this otherwise invisible organization soaks up the mineral kingdom and the forces that are active between individual component elements in the kingdom. I have a plant before me. It is an invisible system of forces that absorbs mineral principles from the mineral kingdom. The result is that the mineral aspect occupies the space also occupied by the invisible system of forces. I see this mineral aspect, though it is merely something the plant, which is not preceptible to the senses, has absorbed. That is how it is even with a plant. When we talk about plants today we are really talking only of the minerals contained within them and not about the plants themselves. It is important that we clearly understand this in the case of a plant, for it also applies to animals and humans, only more so.

During the Old Moon stage, then, human beings did not have this mineral inclusion. Human beings living on the present earth have been made in such a way that they need the mineral kingdom, having absorbed the mineral kingdom and its forces into them, as it were. What significance does this have for human nature? In the first place human beings acquired a mineral body for thinking in images the way they did at the earlier stage. As evolution progressed the mineral human body provided the basis for intellectual thinking. This happened at a relatively late state, from the middle of the 15th century onwards, having been a long time in preparation.

Modern intellectual thinking is based on the fact that human beings have received a mineral body into them. As human beings we need a mineral body first and foremost to be able to think. The older form of thinking in images had been based on what we call the third elemental kingdom. The mineral kingdom had the function to transform this pre-earthly form of thinking into our earthly way of forming ideas on the basis of thought. Within the great scheme of things the spirits with whom human beings had to feel themselves connected, in forming those ideas that were images in the distant past, were then relieved of their function. We will have to picture those spirits rather differently from the way we are accustomed to picture non-human entities. People, even people of good will who may admit that there is more to life than is apparent to the senses, tend to stick too close to the human form. This anthropomorphism takes over whenever people try and create an image in their minds of anything that is above the human sphere. It is easy to accuse Feuerbach and Buechner[1] of being anthropomorphists. We have seen more than enough of this kind of thing. We have seen the legal way of thinking evolve in the Western world, with earthly misdeeds and crimes judged by earthly judges who impose penalties, and so on. The rewards and punishment meted out for sins, i.e. for something belonging to a sphere beyond this earth and seen more as imperfections in the Christian faith, have gradually come to look more like the proceedings in an earthly court of law. The religious ideas of the West have a great deal of human jurisprudence in them. We let the gods mete out punishments of the kind we know earthly courts of law impose. If we truly wish to get beyond the merely human we must firmly decide not to think in entirely human terms. We must think beyond anything anthropomorphic, and that indeed is what really matters in human life. That is the approach we must use if we want to see clearly that the spirits who influenced the thinking in images which human beings had at the time of the Old Moon lost that function in the normal progress of human evolution but are not prepared to accept this with good grace. We might ask why they do not submit to the will of the gods who guide normal progress. They simply do not. We have to accept that as a fact. The original intention was that they should only influence dreams within the human sphere and everything related to dreaming. In the context of today's lecture we refer to them as luciferic spirits. Their proper sphere would be everything that has to do with dreaming and anything related to this. They are not satisfied with this, however. They haunt the human way of thinking that has evolved out of their own sphere, human thinking now bound to the mineral sphere. When we allow anything that normally rules our dreams, the life of the imagination, to enter into our thinking we fall prey in our thinking to luciferic nature, to the influence of spirits that should only have influenced the old form of thinking in images that belonged to the human ancestors. They have retained their power and instead of limiting themselves to our dreaming, our life of the imagination, our creative artistic work, they are constantly trying to influence our thoughts and make them dependent on impulses similar to those that existed in pre-earthly times. Our thinking is still greatly influenced by elements coming from this source, by the luciferic principle.

It is justifiable to ask in all seriousness what powers are these that have such an influence on our thinking. These influences arise from the sphere where we human beings are still rightfully dreaming and rightfully asleep above all else. They come from the sphere of our feelings and emotions. We experience our feelings the way we normally experience dreams and we experience our will the way we experience sleep. There we are still rightly cocooned in a world which becomes a luciferic world as soon as it evolves in our thinking. We therefore will not manage our evolution as human beings properly unless we make the effort to evolve other thoughts as well, thoughts increasingly independent of mere feelings and emotions, of anything arising in us out of dreamlike inner experience even when we are fully awake. Theoretical principles will not help us achieve this, only life itself can do so. We find, however, that the mental habits humankind has acquired put up great resistance to the cultivation of mind and soul that is needed. We must be on the lookout for this resistance. We find that in the present time in particular people are not prepared to listen to anything that does not arise from their own inner prejudices, their feeling of how things should go, their personal preferences. They are not in the habit of listening to anything which in a way has been decided independently of human beings, requiring merely their consent. I should like to give you a brief example which I used on one occasion to explain to someone that there is an important difference with regard to what human beings are thinking.

Many years ago I gave a lecture in a town in southern Germany—today it is no longer in southern Germany—on the wisdom taught in the Christian faith.[2] As you know, it is always necessary to limit the subject matter presented in a particular lecture and one can only speak within that context. When people hear just a single lecture, such a single lecture will impress one person in one way and another in a different way, particularly if one has been objective and dispassionate in presenting the subject. It certainly would not be possible for anyone to get an idea concerning the total philosophy that lies behind a single lecture if they just listened to that one lecture. If the wisdom taught within the Christian faith is the subject for example, it will of course be impossible to conclude from the contents of the lecture what the speaker thinks about the connection between light and electricity, say. It is therefore possible for something to happen the way it did on that occasion. I spoke about the wisdom taught within the Christian faith and two Roman Catholic priests were in the audience. They came up to me afterwards and said: 'No objection can be raised to what you have been saying'—this by the way was many years ago now—'but we have to say that whilst it is true that we say the same thing we do say it in such a way the everybody can understand it'. My reply was: 'Reverend fathers, surely it is like this: You or I may have some kind of inner feeling that we are speaking for everybody, but that is not the point, for that is a subjective feeling. After all it is perfectly natural—if we go entirely by our feeling I, too, must believe that I am speaking for everybody, just as you think you do; that is self-evident; otherwise we would do it differently. But we are now living in an age when our belief that something is justifiable does not count. We need to let the facts speak for themselves. We must learn to look to the facts. Subjectively you believe you are speaking for everybody. But now let me ask you about the facts. Does everybody still come to your church? That would show that you are speaking for everybody. You see, I speak to those who do not come to your church to hear you speak. My words are for those who also have the right to hear of the wisdom taught in Christianity.' That is how we must take our orientation from what the facts have to tell.

It is necessary for us to tear ourselves away from our subjective feelings. If we do not do so the luciferic element will enter into our thinking. We would not have gone through the truly dreadful campaign of untruthfulness that has gone around the world in the last five years, the final consequence of something that has long been in preparation, if people had learned to pay rightful attention to what the facts have to tell and not to their emotions, with nationalists the worst in stirring up such emotions.

On the one hand there is the absolute necessity today to do something about our thinking and to comply even if something goes against the grain. On the other hand people dislike having to be so true to reality that one looks to the facts for guidance.

We shall not be able to attain to the higher worlds and the knowledge to be gained there if we do no train ourselves in rigid adherence to the facts of the external world. Once you have got at least to some extent into the habit of liking to hear the facts you will often suffer tortures when people of the present age want to tell you something. Very often the kind of thing you hear people say is: 'Oh, someone said something and that was frightful, quite terrible!' 'Terrible in what way? You say is was terrible but that only tells me how you felt about it. I really want to hear exactly what it was.' 'Well, it really was terrible what was said there....' And these people simply do not understand. All the time they want to describe their subjective feelings concerning the matter, whilst you want to hear an objective report of what they actually saw. It is especially when people tell you something someone else has told them, that it is quite impossible to tell if they are simply passing on what they have heard or if they have actually looked into the matter they are talking about. This is an area where one has to remind people again and again that truthfulness concerning the knowledge to be found in supersensible spheres can only be achieved if we train ourselves as far as possible to adhere closely to the facts in the sense-perceptible world. That is the only way in which human beings can overcome the luciferic elements that stream into their thoughts—by learning to base ourselves on the facts.

On the one hand mankind is open to luciferic influences, on the other to ahrimanic influences. It had to be said that thinking here on earth evolved from earlier stages of human soul life when human beings absorbed a mineral body, as it were. This mineral body is indeed the organ for the earthly way of thinking. It does however bring it predominantly into the sphere of the powers we call ahrimanic.

We can of course become aware of the need to base ourselves on the facts, on a real world that will get us out of the habit of being swayed by our subjective emotions. We must not, however, fall prey to the kind of thinking that is nothing but an inner activity arising from the mineral body. Here we come upon a truth that many people find highly unpalatable.

You know how some are idealists or spiritualists and others are materialists. There is plenty of discussion in the world as to which is the right approach, spiritualism or materialism. All these debates are of no value whatsoever for certain regions of the human organization. Human beings can develop in two ways. We can use the mineral body we have absorbed into ourselves as the instrument for our thinking, and indeed we have to use it, otherwise we would merely be dreaming. But we can also rise beyond this instrument in our thoughts; we can develop a spiritual point of view, spiritual vision. If we do this we will of course have been thinking with the aid of our material organization, but we will have used this to reach a further stage of human development, ascending to the world of the spirit as a result. On the other hand we can stop at the point where as earth beings we let our mineral body do the thinking. It is perfectly able to do so. That in fact is the danger, and materialism cannot be said to be wrong in its views, particularly where thinking is concerned. This mineral body is no mere photographic print. It is able to think for itself, though its thinking is subject to the limits of life on earth. We need to raise the experience our mineral body is able to give us into the spheres that lie beyond sensory perception.

It is therefore possible to say that it may indeed be true that human thoughts are merely something exuded by the human mineral organization. That may indeed be right, but human beings must first do it right.

Human beings have the freedom to develop on earth in such a way that they are merely the product of matter. Animals cannot do this; they do not get to the point where mineral inclusion leads to the development of thinking activity. Animals cannot choose to prove the truth of the materialistic point of view. Human beings are at liberty to prove the truth of the materialistic point of view; all it needs is the will to do so out of a materialistic attitude to life.

Human freedom is such that people are indeed free to make materialism come true for the human kingdom, that is, they can take a course that will lead to human beings on earth concerning themselves only with material things. Fundamentally speaking, therefore, it is a matter of choice if we become materialists. If we are strong enough to bring to realization what people are told is a materialistic attitude then this attitude will be made to come true by human beings.

This influence on human beings comes from ahrimanic powers. They want to keep everything connected with Earth evolution at the point which has been reached for human beings by that very Earth evolution—that is the point of having a mineral organization. They want to make human beings perfect, but only as far as their mineral organization is concerned. The luciferic powers want to keep human beings, who now have acquired a mineral organization, at the earlier stage that was right for them before they acquired a mineral organization. So we have two powers pulling at the traces, luciferic and ahrimanic powers. The luciferic spirits want to get human beings to a point where they finally cast off their mineralized bodies and go through an evolution that has no relevance in earth life and has merely been an episode in earth life. The luciferic spirits aim for the gradual elimination of everything relating to the earth from the whole evolution of mankind. The ahrimanic spirits aim to take firm hold of this earthly, mineral aspect of human beings, isolate it from progressive evolution and let it stand on its own. That is how luciferic and ahrimanic spirits are pulling in different directions.

It is absolutely vital that having presented the large outline we now come to apply this to ordinary everyday life. We do not consider a U-shaped bar of iron to be a horse-shoe when it is in fact a magnet. In the same way we really should not consider human life to be entirely the way it may appear on the outside. If you shoe a horse with magnets you fail to realize that a magnet has more to it than a horse-shoe. Yet it happens quite often nowadays that people speak of human life exactly like someone who shoes his horse with magnets rather than with horse-shoes. People have no hesitation in speaking of positive and negative electricity in the inorganic sphere, or of positive and negative magnetism, yet they hesitate to speak of luciferic and ahrimanic elements in human life. These are just as effective in human life as positive and negative magnetism are in the inorganic sphere. It is just that the idea of positive and negative magnetism is more easily understood. It does not take as much effort to grasp it as it does to grasp the idea that there are luciferic and ahrimanic elements. That is also the reason why we shall only learn to deal with the empty talk one hears today, empty talk that turns into lies, by knowing that it is luciferic by nature.

Similarly we shall only learn to deal with everything that shows itself here and there as the materialistic point of view by knowing that it is ahrimanic by nature. In future mere external characterization will not get us anywhere when we want to understand human life; all we would be doing is talk around the subject and commit the most stupid of errors when we try and apply such ideas to real life. One thing we would not be doing is to see human life in such a way that social impulses can be gained from our knowledge of human institutions. This has a very much to do with the utter seriousness required when looking at everything connected with evolutionary trends where humankind is concerned. We cannot gain understanding of the life we are now living unless we raise our vision from earthly concerns to spheres beyond this earth. There is a particular point to this.

Looking back into earlier stages of human evolution—though not as far back as those I have spoken of earlier—people generally base themselves on such historical documents as are available. There are historians—well-known names—who say that the history of humankind is made up of everything to be found in the written records. If you start from such a definition of history, like the historian Leopold von Ranke, you will obviously arrive at a particular kind of history. The art of writing is itself part of history, however, it has evolved from something else, and in real terms one cannot do anything with this kind of definition.

We need only go back as far as Chaldean-Babylonian times, to ancient Egyptian times, and we shall find that at that period of human evolution human beings still related to the cosmos in a very different way. People today have no real idea of what it meant to connect one's life to the course of the stars, the planets, and their position relative to the fixed stars of the zodiac. These things have become an empty abstraction nowadays. Do you think a modern astrologer delving into ancient astrological writings to compile his horoscopes—if at least he does search through the old writings, and does not produce new ones; the new ones are terrible!—has even the slightest idea of the living connection which the ancient Egyptians and Chaldeans felt to exist between human beings and the movements and positions of the stars viewed from the earth? Everything is different today. It has to be said that an important part of human evolution since those times has been the narrowing down of human awareness to the physical world. What did those Egyptians know of the earth? It was the ground under their feet. They knew more about the heavens. They moved in the vertical in gaining their experience. The ancient Greeks did not yet go into the horizontal either; they, too, gained their experience by going vertically. The vertical came to be reduced as the horizontal started to spread. The maximun limitation human beings experienced in their knowledge of the heavens came with the great increase in knowledge of the earth that came when men sailed around the globe and found that having sailed away to the west they would return from the east. It was necessary for human understanding in the vertical direction to become obscured. Human beings had to be isolated from the universe so that they could find within themselves the only power that can lead to human freedom. Moral impulses will arise out of this human freedom in their turn.

Human beings therefore no longer relate to the spheres beyond the earth in the vertical fashion the ancient Greeks and Chaldeans did. We have had the training that only a horizontal surface can give and must now ascend again in moral, ethical terms. We must learn how human life is influenced by powers that do not show themselves in the course taken by the world that exists outside us. Those are the luciferic and ahrimanic powers.

People tend to put their minds to other things, however, and sometimes I also have to tell you something relating to our spiritual movement that takes its orientation in anthroposophy. This has accepted the task of working out of the full seriousness the time demands and listening to the language spoken from the cosmos beyond this earth, as it were, a language which tells us that we must once again come to see the way the human being is connected with the whole cosmos. Again and again, however, things make themselves heard in this work—please forgive the abrupt change of subject—which even today draw attention to some very peculiar points of view taken by people who oppose our aims of furthering the progress of mankind. Let me read you a passage from a letter that is really typical. As I said, please forgive the abrupt change of subject but we are obliged to inform you of all kinds of things that are going on at the present time with the purpose of undermining and destroying this movement which endeavours to take up the challenge of the present age.

There is someone in Norway[3] who had made it his task to destroy our movement. To assure himself that he has a right to do so, this man is writing to leading figures—that is how one does these things nowadays. He wrote to a publication called *Politisch-anthropologische Monatsschrift* [Political Anthropological Monthly]. This journal sent him the following information: 'Dr Steiner is a Jew of the purest water. He is connected with the Zionists, indeed associated with them, and works for the Entente.' The editor added that they—i.e. people of this kind—'have had their eye on him for some time.'

I just wanted to tell you this in conclusion, as yet another case among the many one gets today, with a new one coming up almost daily. That is the attitude anthropologists are now taking to the efforts being made in the anthroposophical field.

Stuttgart, 7 March 1920

It has been said on a number of occasions, and also two days ago when I presented the subject from a slightly different point of view, that it is important for us to consider the evolution of the human race in the light of spiritual science and grow aware of the gravity of the present moment. We shall then have to act out of our realization of the gravity of the situation, irrespective of our position in life.

Today I should like to add some further building stones to an edifice that seen in its entirety can show us the present-day tenor of the human mind and spirit and how we shall have to work for the further progress of humankind by taking this state of mind and spirit as our basis. To begin with let us refer to things which in the main are already known to us.

We know that the human race in its present state of civilization has by and large descended from the human race that evolved before disaster befell the continent of Atlantis. It has been said on a number of occasions that Atlantis occupied an area between present-day Europe, Africa and America that is today covered by the Atlantic Ocean. We know that under the influence of that disaster—in the course of its preparation and later as it proceeded—the peoples of that time migrated first in an eastward direction, populating Europe and then Asia as they moved on, and that the European and Asian peoples of the present day are in fact the descendants of the peoples of Atlantis. We also know that civilization then took the opposite route and people coming to colonize Europe brought civilization with them, as it were: cultural contents that had first been achieved in Asia. These then spread further from a number of centres in Europe. Thus I would say that the physical basis for modern civilization is provided by the peoples of Europe and Asia, descendants of the ancient Atlantean race that moved from the west to the east. Civilization itself however moved from east to west. These two movements can only be properly distinguished on the basis of spiritual-scientific investigation. The two are confused in conventional athropology and it is not realized that only the culture, the civilization, has been transplanted from east to west, whilst the physical basis comes from migrations that proceded from west to east.

People always have some relationship to the locality where they live. We relate in some way to the soil under our feet, to everything this soil produces, to the way the soil comes to expression in climatic conditions and provides a habitat. You can conclude from this—and spiritual science fully confirms it—that the peoples who went further into Asia in the course of those post-Atlantean migrations inevitably had to develop in a different way from those who had remained in Europe. In ordinary terms this means that the soil of Europe had a different effect on the descendants of the Atlanteans than the soil of Asia. In a way, we can define the difference between the populations of Asia and of Europe. The difference is that particularly during the earliest periods of post-Atlantean civilization, during the 9th, 8th, 7th and 6th millenium BC and the millenia that followed, the people of Asia adopted intellectual thinking, thinking as we know it, in a different way. This type of thinking did not fully emerge until the 15th century, as I said on the last occasion, but it was in preparation for centuries and indeed millenia before that.

This form of thinking as we know it today only developed in very recent times, assuming its true character in intellectual thinking as the soul itself became inwardly active. But the whole of our evolution, particularly in post-Atlantean times, has been tending towards this intellectual approach. It is significant that the post-Atlantean population of Asia accepted all that we may call intellectual more into its soul elements. We can say that due to local conditions the peoples of Asia were specifically predestined for the early stages of intelligence to enter into their souls. The most remarkable aspect of Asian civilization is that the soul element as such became the instrument for adopting the intellectual principle.

It was different with the people who had remained in Europe. Quite specifically the situation was that physical development, the physical organization that later on was to become the real instrument of intellectual development, evolved in such a way that even at an earlier stage it became the essential characteristic of these peoples, constituting itself in a way that was particularly suited to be the vehicle for the intellectual principle. If we therefore wish to characterize the descendants of the Atlanteans' earliest descendants, that is ourselves, we have to say that the Asian peoples got more into the habit of thinking with their souls; the Europeans got into the habit of thinking more with their bodies. That is in fact the major difference between the civilizations of Asian and Europe. If you want to show up the clear difference which exists between the kind of intelligence apparent in the Vedic writings or Vedantic philosophy and other cultural streams in Asia compared to European culture you have to say to yourselves: Asians are thinking more with their souls, Europeans more with their bodies.

The people of Asia may thus be said to have taken the intellecutal element into a higher aspect of their human nature, with the result that an advanced civilization developed much earlier. This however was a civilization of the soul that had fewer abstract concepts, a culture that found its own ways to higher things, using the human soul and spirit to reach the soul and spirit of the world without resorting to abstract concepts. That is where the spiritual nature of Asian civilization lies—inasmuch as it is essentially a civilization based on soul qualities. The peoples of Asia largely left their bodies unused when it came to thinking; they merely carried their bodies with them through life on earth. The life of the mind was nurtured entirely at soul level. You cannot understand the peculiar nature of Asian culture unless you look at it from this point of view.

Europeans were basing their thinking more and more on the physical body. That is also why the foundations were more strongly laid among them than in Asia for a culture in which freedom can be the central principle. The people of Asia, endowed with intelligence at soul level, still were more part of the whole cosmic organism. The human body specifically isolates itself from the rest of the cosmic organism. Using it as the instrument for our intellectual life we become more independent, though this independence is more bound up with the body than is the case with the people of Asia who have developed intelligence within the soul principle and are consequently less independent.

As the time approached in the history of humankind that was to bring the Mystery of Golgotha, an advanced culture of soul and spirit had evolved in Asia. At the time of the Mystery of Golgotha it had already reached its culmination and was in the early stages of decline. Do not let us deceive ourselves: European ideas do not make it easy to grasp the great culture which had grown out of the soul and spirit of the Asian peoples. When people who are throughly European in their way of thinking, people for whom the physical body is the instrument of thinking, want to get Europeans to appreciate Asian ideas, as Deussen[4] has done, for example, the outcome in no way represents the contents of Asian civilization of soul and spirit, for everything alive in it has been translated into European thought. It has even happened that interpretations of certain spiritual streams in India caused a sensation in Europe—those published by von Garbe,[5] for instance, yet it was nothing more than Euopean materialism producing a garbled translation of Asian soul and spirit culture. Publications of this kind contain a trace of the real spirit of ancient Asia. It is necessary to point this out very firmly because, as I have said before, belief in authority has reached an extreme degree and people really have nothing in them that permits them to acknowledge the validity of something, except the fact that it has been written by university professors. There is of course no real inner reason why Deussen's or Garbe's botchwork should be considered important in any way, except that there is this belief in authority in Europe which is going sadly astray. People are no longer in a position even to find any kind of inner reason; they merely believe one thing or another to be right because some outer authority says so. It does not help to avoid saying the truth about these things—even if it means making more enemies—for the gravity of the present situation absolutely demands that there shall be no compromise where certain things are concerned and that the truth must be clearly stated.

The advanced culture of the spirit in Asia was already to some extent in decline when the event of Golgotha occurred. This event of Golgotha—it cannot be sufficiently stressed—was first of all taken in and understood by minds that were the product of Asian culture. It is important to distinguish between the Mystery of Golgotha as a historical event that happened in the Near East at the beginning of Christian era and the notions people have of this Mystery of Golgotha. At the time when the event occurred, Europe did not have the capacity to grasp it fully, for it was an event that could only be grasped in soul and spirit. European civilization, however, had spread by using physical matter as its instrument. The event which occurred at the beginning of our Christian era could not be directly grasped in a civilization based on physical and material things. Asian civilization on the other hand had an intellecutal life based on soul and spirit and out of this was able to find concepts with which to grasp the event of Golgotha. The event that happened in Palestine was thus poured into the conceptual world of the Orient. In that form it travelled westward through Greece and Italy and came to Europe as a tradition.

People can be given something in an external way that they cannot yet grasp in their hearts and minds. Things may come to them in the form of a tradition or through the written word. Europe initially was given the explanation, its understanding of the Mystery of Golgotha, out of the oriental tradition. Christianity was understood in the light of oriental wisdom, a wisdom of soul and spirit that was truly great at a time when the Mystery of Golgotha, and the way Christ related to the whole of Earth evolution, were still perceived gnostically. It dwindled more and more as Europeans were increasingly blending their own unique characteristic into this tradition. They had to bring their particular characteristic of an intellectual life bound to the physical body into the way they saw these things. The following happened, particularly in Europe: In early times the human bodies of Europeans were very much the instrument of their kind of elementary intellectual thinking, but then this body gradually began to die. Physical evolution of European humanity until the 15th century and even to this day consisted in the physical body growing more and more dead. Our physical bodies are growing denser and denser and more and more bony. We cannot demonstrate this with the methods of ordinary anatomy and physiology, but it is true. We no longer have bodies as inwardly alive as those of people living in the 1st, 3rd and even the 10th and 11th centuries. Our European bodies of today have grown bony, paralyzed, compared to those ancient bodies that were inwardly alive. Thus you have on the one hand a tradition designed for the soul and spirit of Asian people who preserved the ecclesiastical creeds, and on the other hand a more and more European body that increasingly felt those Asian traditions to be alien and in the end no longer found itself able to take in the ideas coming from Asia.

From the middle of the 15th century onwards the influence of the bony European body has been such that in the end that old tradition only survived in empty outer phrases among religious communities. For many centuries the tradition had been so much alive that little regard was paid to the Gospels and people took their cue from life itself. As the European body came to die off people felt impelled to say: Let us cast off the old tradition; we want to put our faith only in the Word, the Word as it is written. People believe they have the Word when in fact they only have a poor translation of it. It gradually came about—though no one is willing to admit it—that really all one had was the outer shell of the Word of old that once held within it the tidings of the Mystery of Golgotha in the garb of oriental wisdom, a wisdom of soul and spirit.

This oriental wisdom is little understood by the people who generally interpret or translate the Gospels; they understand little, if any of it. The point is that it is necessary to see the Mystery of Golgotha in a new light. However, unless we Europeans get beyond what a dying physical body is able to give we will be unable to do so. We must develop through spiritual science and come to grasp the spiritual world in a way where we are independent of this body. Our future salvation entirely depends on our ability to grasp the spiritual world in this way, independently of our physical bodies, going straight for the spirit. It will have to be different in essence from the oriental culture of soul and spirit, which came as though of its own accord as human beings evolved. Europeans of the present time will need to achieve it by their own efforts. They will have to nurture spiritual science. They will have to create an educational system where from the bottom rung upwards spiritual science is not presented as a theory but flows into everything we do as we teach and train the children. Spiritual science should also flow into higher education and should be alive in everything connected with art, literature and so on, everything that is our common cultural life. This European culture must provide for the nuturing of spiritual science itself. On the basis of such a spiritual science the Mystery of Golgotha will then be seen in a new light. We shall have to say that those were the old times when the Mystery of Golgotha was only interpreted in the light of the wisdom of spirit and soul that belonged to the Orient. A new wisdom will have to grasp the Mystery of Golgotha in a new and living way.

We have spoken about these things quite often and in many respects. It is necessary, however, that they take hold of our soul from all sides. It is necessary that we come to experience a seriousness that absolutely fills our hearts and minds with the realization that new insight has to be gained into the Mystery of Golgotha. This is something that makes the seriousness that is required particularly in Central Europe even more austere.

Looking with more profound insight at what has become cultural life in the second half of the 18th and first half of the 19th century particularly in Central Europe you really have to say this: The bodies of people in Central Europe were already dying, but they still were so much alive that the people were able to rise to a world of ideas more alive than ever seen before in the evolution of humankind. Nowhere else did human minds rise to abstract ideas in such a way that whilst living in these abstract ideas one was not in the sphere of death but in the sphere of life. That was achieved in Goetheanism, for instance, and by German idealist philosophers. It is not something to be found anywhere else in human evolution. It was also in a way a culmination, one merely has to get this quite clear in one's mind. People today no longer want to know how Schelling, for instance, to take just one of the Goetheanists, moved in a sphere of abstract thoughts and yet, whilst speaking in quite abstract terms, was alive in the way he moved in the sphere of abstract thoughts: as alive as people usually are when they speak of food and drink. The same applies to Fichte. This was an area of human evolution where we are especially aware of an ability to descend into the sphere of concepts and ideas in a way that was very much alive. Something quite special exists therefore for this Central European population, special in the whole context of human evolution in more recent times. They have their own characteristics that enable them in particular to take up the vocation of humankind for the present day: namely, to enter into spirituality again. These characteristics only came to be submerged beneath other things in the second half of the 19th century.

It is terribly painful to be aware of a very sleepy human being in Central Europe today walking over the graves of Lessing and Goethe and Herder and Schelling. This human being considers its role to be that of a soul asleep. If we were to pick up the thread of the writings and thoughts of those great minds, not in an external way but entering into the spirit in which they wrote, we would find the element that can raise Europe to the heights. Europe cannot be made to rise to the heights by Gospel words repeated parrot-fashion in the churches that no one understands. Europe can only be made to rise if people seek to grasp the spiritual worlds by developing further what Herder, Goethe and others have been working towards. There is however hardly any awareness of this at the present time. It is a sad sign of the times for example that in a cultural community which possesses treasures like Fichte's 'Goal and Purpose of the Human Being', Schelling's *Bruno* and Schiller's *Letters on Aesthetic Education*[6], and there are many more I could mention; that in such a cultural community people could follow a trend that led to the inane and superficial Americanisms of Raph Waldo Trine[7] and the like. We have things that are much more sublime but we let them sleep and turn to other things.

The further we penetrate into the actual life of the mind and spirit the more it becomes apparent that something new is emerging in the life of humankind today. Central Europeans are far from understood by Western Europeans; Western Europeans are far from understood by Central Europeans, even in ordinary life. People are not aware of this, however. They think they understand each other. They do not realize that they are not communicating their thoughts. I am not referring to the way Americans and Europeans fail to communicate, but Central and Western Europeans. You come across some odd things in this respect.

The last time I was here I told you that vilification is rife not only within Germany but also outside its borders.[8] I told you about this man Ferrière[9], for instance, who spread one of the strangest tales in a Swiss-Belgian journal, saying that it was of course generally known that I was 'Rasputin' to William II[10] and had a major share in all the bad advice William II was given in those terrible days. This slanderous story came to be widely known particularly in French-speaking Switzerland and I therefore defended myself by writing down the truth of the matter, stating the bare facts. I said that I had only ever seen the former emperor briefly and from a distance, had never spoken with him at all and never sought to contact him even through others. These are the bare facts I stated in a letter to Dr Boos[11] who then gave Mr Ferrière the necessary set-down. The matter was published in the journal in question together with Ferrière's reply. This went more or less as follows: Once again the great difference between the Latin and the Germanic mind is demonstrated. The Germanic mind takes everything so seriously. 'My readers', Ferrière wrote, 'will of course not have been deceived; they will have realized that what I wrote was intended to be *plaisanterie* and not *méchanceté*[12]. Apart from that let me state that it is possible to learn that something we may have heard from people whom we think we can believe need nevertheless not be true, even if it is a widely believed rumour. I am taking note of this.' And so on.

That was the elegant reply the 'Latin mind' was able to give, with a *plaisanterie* concerning the Germanic mind. At least one has the satisfaction that these things have come to the fore; very often they are not even noticed.

They assume even greater significance where a more profound view is taken of the world, at the point where they relate to initiation knowledge and everything connected with this. This is a sphere where it is indeed necessary to mention these things just for once, though some people consider it highly dangerous to touch on them even today. I want to talk to you today about a matter that in the opinion of representatives of initiation knowledge, Western representatives in particular, should not be discussed.

Western representatives of initiation knowledge will tell you again and again that it simply will not do for anyone to spread initiation knowledge they have gained for themselves. You will find that when genuine initiates in the West present initiation knowledge in books available to the public they always deny having personal experience of the things of which they are writing. You will find that it is quite typical—such things have appeared particularly in America—to have a preface, that is part of the whole technique, which says the following: 'None of these things are my own, of course, for if they were just my own I would not mention them'. Take a look, you will find this kind of thing in many documents published particularly by

Western initiates. If you ask why it is done like this you will be given an answer that within certain limits is certainly true for Western initiation science. You will be told that anyone learning something directly from the spiritual world, who knows the secrets of the spiritual world, cannot tell another person that he has it from personal experience—these will be the words used to answer the question—for if he betrays the fact that he has initiation knowledge from personal experience he becomes dependent for life on the person to whom he betrayed his secret.

This attitude has its roots in the essential nature of Western initiation science. The effect is that anything to do with initiation is discussed in a very superficial way among Western initiates in their societies, and that there are indeed initiates moving around among Western humanity of whom nobody knows that they are initiates. This is an attitude that has to be overcome in the new age; it cannot hold true in Central Europe, and the spirit which must arise in Central Europe will have to fight this attitude. It will have to fight it by coming to understand the Mystery of Golgotha in the new and spiritual way I have talked about. It will have to come to understand the presence of the Christ in human life.

Here lies a major secret. The usual initiation knowledge in Western countries is far removed from Christianity; otherwise the Theosophical Society would not have excluded or caricatured the Christian faith and presented a purely oriental, pre-Christian Indian wisdom as something new. It is a peculiar characteristic of this Western initiation knowledge that its initiates only have something of their initiation if they have at least one pupil who reiterates their ideas. There is no point whatsoever in having initiation knowledge just for oneself. If your eyes look straight ahead you will not see a single object. In the same way you will not encounter your own ideas of the spirit as a Western initiate unless you can see your own ideas repeated by someone else. There are all kinds of indications of this, but it is not properly realized.

Indeed, if this is the case then it is true that someone who betrays to another person the fact that he is an initiate will be in the power of that other person for the rest of his life. The other could then refuse to serve him and say: I am not going to repeat your ideas. That implies some degree of dependence. That essentially is a characteristic of the initiation knowledge I have frequently referred to in other respects, referring to it as the dominant initiation science in the West.

There is only one way out of this dependence on one's followers and that is to be in communion with Christ, who can truly be found on earth since the Mystery of Golgotha. We are not then in communion with a human being who is not perceptible to the senses but with the first among brothers who has come among men, with the living Christ walking among us. If we are in a communion with Christ the way we had to be in communion with other persons in pre-Christian initiation, we need not be afraid to share our own wisdom with our fellow human beings. There is no other way in the present time in which original initiation wisdom can be directly communicated than by being in communion with Christ. There is no other way. A genuine initiation wisdom of the present age will have to look for such communion with Christ.

If this initiation wisdom were not there to be found we could make no progress in social understanding. It is no longer possible to evolve social ideas nowadays unless we base ourselves on initiation. Yet we have need of social ideas. A social system born wholly out of Western initiation wisdom would depend on that initiation wisdom being kept secret even at its lowest levels—certain higher levels cannot be made known today because people must have the necessary preparation. Keeping things secret in this way is not compatible however with the principle of people being equal, a principle modern Europeans and indeed the whole civilized world consider important today. So you see that exactly when it comes to initiation wisdom a colossal difference shows itself between the Central European and the Western mind. The difference becomes even more apparent in the case of initiation wisdom than in the situation where people talk above each others heads in the present time and believe humankind can be brought to an abstract uniformity. That cannot be done. Human beings are differentiated and this differentiation shows itself particularly if one takes a more profound look at initiation knowledge. This is an important subject and it will no doubt be necessary for me to explain it in more detail during the time I am here. When it comes to genuine spiritual insight one simply cannot be slipshod about things, and a lack of seriousness concerning the truth is unacceptable. It simply will not do. Truthfulness is of the essence.

Stuttgart, 9 March 1920

There are a few things I want to add to the points we have been considering. They may help to make some of the ideas on which we must base our actions more real. I am looking for ideas that are less abstract than the vast majority of ideas by which people allow themselves to be governed today. We really need such concrete ideas, for they are the only ones that enter into the realm of feeling for human beings, and therefore into real life. They are the only ideas to fire the human will and human actions.

Looking at the world today we should really consider the most striking characteristic of social life in the civilized world to be that the smaller communities of past times have given way to quite large human communities. We need not go far back in human evolution to find that social communities extended only over limited territories. The civic communities of towns formed a relative whole, and fundamentally speaking it is only now, in quite recent times, that large empires have arisen, that the empire of English-speaking peoples has come about—I have characterized this a number of times. None of us should have any illusions concerning the consequences, particularly in Central Europe. It needs the point of view of spiritual science, however, to get the right ideas about these things, ideas that fully relate to reality. The spiritual-scientific point of view makes us go back to earlier stages of human development to see that then, too, people formed certain kinds of communities, though these should not be called 'states'—as I have said on a number of occasions—for that would cause tremendous confusion. Instead, let us find some other, more neutral term. Let us say that 'realms' arose. Such realms were ruled by individuals, or by particular groups. Subsequently states developed out of this, and today states are taken so much for granted that no one would think of going against them—at least in certain areas no one would go against them.

What is worse, they are so much taken for granted that people are not even inclined to think about them.

Behind this, however, lies something that unites human beings in their inner soul life with the spiritual, the divine principle, as it came to be called during different stages of earth evolution.

If we go back to prehistoric times, times that only partly extend into historical times, we find that in those prehistoric times the idea of a ruler of the realm, as we may call it—whatever words we use do not really fit those earlier ideas—was quite different from what we take it to mean today. The idea of the ruler of an earthly realm came very close to what people knew to be their idea of a god. These things inevitably must seem highly paradoxical to modern minds, though that is only because modern minds are little inclined to take serious consideration of things that existed during the past in human evolution and do not fit in with the way of thinking that has become customary in Western Europe and in its appendage, America, over the last three or four hundred years.

Of course the way a ruler of the realm was introduced to his office, at least in many empires, was very different in those early partly prehistoric times. We need only go back as far as ancient Egypt, meaning the earlier, partly prehistoric times of ancient Egypt, or as far as Chaldea, and we shall find that it was considered a matter of course that regents were prepared for their office by the forerunners of our present-day priests. People had quite concrete ideas as to how a ruler should be prepared for office by the priesthood and its institutions. They felt that with this kind of preparation the person called to be regent truly became what the Chinese, still having a faint notion of this, called the Son of Heaven. There was an awareness that someone called to rule over some region had to be made a kind of Son of Heaven. What was in people's minds was however something quite different from the one and only idea we have today when we speak of training a person or preparing them for something. You can go to great lengths to explain that one should not train people for some office or other in this world by merely implanting intellectual knowledge into their souls, but that the whole person needs to be developed; practically all our ideas today on development, education and so on tend to be abstract to an extreme degree. People have the idea that only some aspect or other of the human being should be changed or transformed to advance him in his training, his preparation for some office. No one thinks that development should be such that the individual undergoes a complete change. Above all no one thinks that something objective should enter into the soul of that individual, something that was not there before. No one has that idea. I could characterize this more or less as follows: I am talking to someone who is the product of the natural and social life of the present day. He tells me this and that, I tell him this or that. The person who speaks to me bears a name: he is the product of the usual natural and social background that people have today. The same applies to me. That is really almost the only way in which we behave towards each other nowadays, the way in which we look at each other.

In the times of which I have been speaking that would have been a very alien notion. It was above all alien to people called to hold important offices, to be leaders within the human community. The external natural background—family origins, father, mother, grandfather, grandmother and so on—was of no real concern if the people concerned had been properly prepared for their office. The things we look for and find in present-day individuals who have been raised to the highest spheres were then of no account. People felt that if they spoke to someone who had been properly trained in this respect it was not the ordinary ego that spoke to them: i.e. an ego born in some place or another, bearing the imprint of some social background or other. Instead they felt that something was speaking to them that had been made to come down from spiritual heights to take up its abode in a human individual thanks to the preparation and training given in the mystery cult. This must of course sound incredibly strange to present-day people. It is however necessary to stop harbouring confused notions about these things and to form ideas that have their basis in truth.

The idea was that education—not all training but the training of people called to high office—should enable spirits from the higher hierarchies to speak through these individuals, using them as their instruments. Those instruments were prepared by training, so that spirits of the higher hierarchies would be able to speak through them. There was general awareness of this, particularly when the population at large came to form an opinion about the identity of their ruler.

Remnants of this still survive, for instance in the title Son of Heaven for the ruler of China. That was the level of human awareness in earliest Egyptian and Chaldean times. Spiritual science has established this. To the people at large their ruler was God. Basically they had no other concept of divinity. The preparation of the ruler had been such that the outer physical form was nothing, it merely made it possible for a god to move among human beings. The earliest inhabitants of what was later to become the kingdom of Egypt quite naturally accepted the fact that they were ruled by gods who walked on earth in human form. In this respect the earliest social awareness of human beings was entirely realistic. There was no recognition of a separate world beyond, of a separate spiritual world. The spiritual world existed in the same place as the world within which people moved on earth. In this world, where human beings walked the earth, not only ordinary human individuals were walking about in physical form but also gods. The divine world was right among them, made absolute and visible under the conditions regularly created through the mystery cult. When such a ruler wanted something, decreed something, it was a god who wanted it. To the minds of earliest humankind during that partly prehistoric period it would have been pointless to question whether something decreed by their ruler should or should not happen; it was after all a 'god' who wanted it.

Earliest humanity thus connected the spiritual hierarchies with everything that happened on earth. Those hierarchies were there in their midst; they were not something to which one first has to ascend by some kind of spiritual, inner means. No, they were present in the mysteries as the training given to physical bodies found suitable for preparation as dwelling places for spirits of the higher hierarchies, so that these might walk among human beings and be their rulers.

This may seem strange to modern minds, but modern minds will finally have to leave behind the narrow-minded views they hold today, ideas only three or four hundred years old as we know them today, and take a wider view. We cannot develop and think ahead to the future unless we broaden the tunnel vision which has evolved in almost every sphere of life. We must expand the time horizons we survey and consider larger evolutionary time spans than present-day history normally covers.

The things of the past, things that existed in historical and prehistoric evolution, do of course give way to other things as time progresses, but in certain areas they are retained. They are often retained by becoming external, continuing in an outer form and losing their inner meaning. The awareness of the godlike nature of the ruler that was a feature of earliest imperialism still comes up here or there in the present age, except that it no longer has any meaning, since mankind progresses and does not stand still.

Not long ago a Roman Catholic bishop addressed a pastoral to his diocese[13] in which he stated nothing more and nothing less than that a Roman Catholic priest conducting an act of worship was more powerful than Christ Jesus himself. Acting as the celebrant, the priest coerced Christ Jesus, the god of Christianity, to enter into the physical world as the priest performed the act of transubstantiation. The god might be willing or not, the act of transubstantiation forced him to take the route prescribed by the priest. It is really true that very recently a pastoral referred to the sublime power of the earth-born 'priest god' over the 'inferior god' who descended from cosmic heights and walked on the earth in the flesh of Jesus. Things like this have their origin in older times and have lost their meaning in the present age. Some people representing certain confessions know very well, of course, why they keep throwing such things into human minds. They have become just as meaningless as the words modern rulers write in albums: The king's wishes are the supreme law.[14] These things have happened in our times. Humanity, fast asleep, has said nothing at all about it and still says nothing now to things going on that bode ill for humankind, things one gets used to, things one does not want to see. Today we are altogether little prepared to take note of major events in human evolution.

That was a first stage in the evolution of human empires: when the ruler was the god. This way of looking at it was still very much alive in Roman times. Whichever way you may look at Nero, as a fool or a bloodhound, for the large majority of the Roman people Nero's dreadful tyranny merely made them marvel that a god could walk on earth in such a guise. Many of the citizens of imperial Rome never doubted that the figure of Nero was that of a god.

A second stage in the evolution of empires came with the transition from a ruler who was a god to one who ruled by the grace of God. During the earliest times of human evolution on the civilized earth the ruler was God. At the second stage the ruler stood for God; he was not indwelt by the god himself but inspired by God, given special grace. Everything he did would succeed because divine power—now no longer within him but in a realm close to the earthly realm—flowed into him, inspired him, filled him, and guided him in all he did.

To describe the essential nature of such a second stage ruler we have to say that the ruler was a symbol. At the first stage the ruler was a divine spirit walking on earth. At the second stage he represented what that spirit signified; he was the sign, the symbol in which the spirit came to expression. The ruler became the image of God.

The principles governing those external social relationships also came to expression in the institutions which became established. In earliest times empires were so constituted that a number of people were governed by a divine spirit. This god would be similar to them in external appearance but utterly different inside. At the second stage we find empires where the leader or leaders represent the god or gods and are symbols for them.

At the early stage of human empires discussion as the whether the ruler, the god, was acting rightly or wrongly was beside the point. At the second stage it began to be possible to think whether something he had done was right or wrong. At the early stage everything the ruler did, thought or said was right, for he was the god. Then, at the second stage, some other spiritual sphere was felt to exist side be side with the earthly realm, one that has the god, the ruler given the grace of God, within it. The power streaming into the earthly realm, giving direction and orientation, was felt to come from that other realm. The institutions and human individuals in the earthly realm were the reflection of something streaming in from the realm of the higher hierarchies.

It is interesting to find out, for example, that Dionysius the Areopagite,[15] also called the pseudo-Dionysius, who was much more genuine than orthodox science imagines, presented the right theory concerning the way human empires were ruled by divine empires so that the conditions and institutions created among humans were a symbol of what existed in the divine realm. Dionysius the Areopagite wrote that there were heavenly hierarchies behind the human hierarchies on this earth. He stated very clearly that the social structure of the priestly hierarchy here on earth, from deacons and archdeacons all the way up to bishops, ought to show that the relationship of deacon to archdeacon is the same as that of angel to archangel, and so on. The earthly hierarchy should truly reflect the heavenly hierarchy. This refers to the second stage of empires. Something was able to evolve that was to govern human ideas until quite recent times. After all there existed in Central Europe until 1806 an institution that in its title gave expression to the way the heavenly and the earthly principle were seen to be one: the Holy Roman Empire, an empire seen to be based on the power of heaven. The words 'of German nationality' were added [to the German title] to show that the empire was also of earthly origin. The way the title evolved it is evident that a whole empire was formed in such a way that it should be seen to be the image of a heavenly insititution.

Such were also the ideas behind St Augustine's *City of God* and Dante's work *On the Monarchy*[16]. If only people were not so limited in their ideas they could take a wider view when reading something like Dante's work and realize that Dante, who after all must be considered a great thinker, still had ideas in the 13th and 14th centuries that are radically different from our modern ideas. If we were to take such things in historical evolution seriously we would give up those narrow ideas that do not even go back as far as Dante but are just a few hundred years old. The ideas used by people nowadays to fill their heads with illusions, wanting to understand history by merely going back as far as ancient Greece, are limited ideas. Yet it is only possible to understand the whole structure of ancient Egypt, for instance, if we know that the ancient gods still walked on earth. In the times that followed gods no longer walked on the earth, but the institutions created on earth had to be an image, a symbol, of the divine world order.

Then something arose for example like the possibility to reflect on the lawfulness of things, to reflect on such things as the fact that the human intellect can arrive at a judgement as to what is lawful and what is not—all this only became possible during the second stage of imperial development. During the earliest stage it was pointless to reflect on what was lawful and what was not. People had to look to what the ruler said, for the god lived in him, he was the god. In the second stage, human judgement could be used to determine that there is something in a spiritual realm next to our own realm that we cannot reach as physical human beings but only as human beings of soul and spirit. Then people no longer believed, as they had believed in earlier times, that the divine could unite with the whole physical human being, that a human being could indeed become a god. At most—using mystical language to define the living truth about public institutions—people believed that the human soul element could unite with the god.

Basically it is true to say that no one nowadays is able to understand the way things were said in works written and published as late as the 13th and 14th centuries unless one knows that the people of that time had quite a different awareness, a feeling that some degree of divine inspiration was alive in those who were called and trained to hold special office. Oddly enough things referring to something rather serious will often become derisory expressions at a later point in time when the evolution of humankind has progressed. Someone saying 'God shapes the back for the burthen' nowadays would say this more or less as a joke. Yet though it may be said today partly as a joke, in the times when empires were at their second stage of development it certainly held true and was to the forefront of people's minds. It applied not only to people but within certain limits also to what was being done. Rituals were made to be such that the actions performed in them reflected what went on in the spiritual realms. The rituals performed were spiritual events reaching across into what went on in the physical world. People very much believed the spiritual realm to be adjoining the physical realm, but they also thought that it extended across into the earthly realm and that the symbol or sign of the spiritual realm was to be found in the earthly realm.

Very gradually people ceased to believe in the validity of this. An age was to follow where this awareness of the connection between earthly and spiritual things was to fade. In the days of Wycliffe, of Huss, [17] people began to dispute things which it would have been unthinkable to dispute before. They were in disagreement on the significance of transubstantiation: whether this ritual act had anything to do with what went on in spiritual worlds. When people begin to disagree about such things, old ideas are coming to an end. People no longer know what to think; yet for centuries, indeed millenia, they had known exactly what to think. It always happens that certain things normal to a particular age continue to play a role in later ages. They are then out of place, anachronistic, luciferic. That is what has happened to the great, far-reaching symbols relating to a particular age when they showed how ritual acts and the like performed on earth were connected with divine and spiritual happenings in the world. Those symbols persisted during later ages and certain secret societies preserved them in a luciferic way. Western secret societies in particular have been preserving such ancient symbols. They are traditional in those societies, though they have lost their real content. On the one hand, then, we see certain secret societies—Freemasons, Jesuit organizations and denominational groups have arisen from these—preserving, in a way, those symbols which only had meaning in an earlier age. On the other hand we see how words preserve ideas that belonged to an earlier age in a basically luciferic way. Words used in everyday life have also lost their original substance, lost the context of a way of thinking when those words were symbols of spiritual things. For the spiritual content is gradually lost and words become empty symbols, signs without meaning.

During a third period, at a third level of empire development, there was no longer any awareness of individuals being given the grace of God, of divine elements entering into earthly events, earthly speech. The spiritual realm was now entirely in the beyond. The opposite of what had existed at the first stage of empire development now held true. During the first stage the god lived on earth, went about in human form. During the third stage one can only think of the god being present in an invisible world that is not perceptible to the senses. Everything people were able to use to express their relationship with the realm of divine spirits lost its meaning. The word 'god' continues to be used. When the word 'god' was spoken in the distant past people were looking for something that appeared in human form, walking among human beings. It is not that human beings in those very early times were materialists. Materialists only became possible once the spiritual realm had been banished beyond the sense-perceptible world.

During the earliest period of human evolution the spiritual world was right there among human beings. There would have been no need for someone living in ancient Egypt during its earliest times to say: The kingdom of the divine is at hand. He would take that to be self-evident. At the time when Christ Jesus appeared among men people first had to be told: 'The Kingdom of the gods cometh not with observation ... for, behold, it is within you.'[18]

We are now living in an age when it would be a nonsense to look to a person for anything but a straightforward development of what he was as a child, a development based on cause and effect. We live in an age when it would be sheer madness for someone to consider himself more than the straightforward further development of what was also there in his childhood. Eight thousand years ago, let us say, something was taken as a matter of course, was the general way of thinking; yet if anyone were to say the same thing today this would merely indicate that they are mad. The realities of those distant times have been reinterpreted in the modern way of thinking into that fictitious tale we call 'history'. This spreads a veil over the radical metamorphosis we are able to dicover when we consider human evolution in the light of truth. The things we often say today, things we reveal in our external life, exist because they once had relevance and were considered to be the truth. We still say things like 'by the grace of God'—people have more or less tried to get out of the habit in recent years, but they have not succeeded very well with this—but we do not know, or pay no attention to the fact, that there was a time when this was a reality to human minds, when it was taken as a matter of course.

Here I am drawing your attention to things that give our public life its meaningless, conventional character. Things we put forward in the words we use, in our customs and indeed the way we judge issues in public life, relate to times when those words, even if they only became part of the vocabulary at a later date—they were modelled on the original language—were formed and used on quite a different basis. The words we use in public life today have been squeezed dry. With some it is immediately apparent, with others it was not apparent for a long time. In the distant past a token was hung upon a human body in magical body in magical rites, transforming it into an important magical aspect of the god walking on earth. This has become something trival in the decorations given to people today. That is the kind of history humankind is unlikely to pursue. Not only words can become empty phrases and lose all meaning, as is the case with the most important words used in public life today; the objects hung around people's necks or pinned to their chests can show similar character in their relation to reality, like a word that is meaningless today but once had sacred meaning and substance to it.

We must realize that initially our evolution was such that an older awareness lost its substance and became empty and conventional. There can be no real new growth in our devastated public life of today unless we do so. We must look for new well-springs that will give real substance again to public life. We have no awareness of gods walking the earth in human form. We must therefore acquire the ability to recognise the spirit not in human form but in the form it has when we rise to spiritual vision. For us the gods no longer descend to sit on physical thrones. We must acquire the spiritual faculties that enable us to ascend in our vision to the thrones where gods are to be found who can only be alive to us in the spirit. We must learn to fill the abstract formulas we use with spiritual contents of our own experience. We must become able to face truths that are deeply disturbing to those who grasp them rightly. We must become able to see things as they are. Sometimes we fail to do so for periods extending over decades.

As Central Europeans we believe ourselves to be part of European civilization. What we should ask ourselves is what it is that has made our inner life, the life of our soul, so full of discord over the last fifty years or even longer. Let me say just one thing. When you look to the West you see in the first instance—we'll leave aside the rest—a nation falling into decadence, the French nation. One thing is important, however, among the French. When a member of this nation said: I am a Frenchman— this is what they have said to themselves for centuries—he said something that was in accord with the external facts; a permissible, truthful declaration made with reference to external life. Any of us who have ever talked to people who were young and German in the first half of the 19th century will be able to confirm the following. Herman Grimm[19] for instance has repeatedly described what it meant, to people who were young when he was young in Germany, for someone to profess himself to be German in public life, not as an empty phrase but in reality. It would have been treason. People were Bavarians, Wurttembergians, Prussians, but to say 'I am German' would make them criminals. In the West there was a point to saying 'I am a Frenchman', people were permitted to be that in external life. It would have meant going to prison or being put beyond the pale in some other way if one had taken it into one's mind to say one was German, i.e. belonged to a united nation. People have forgotten about this now, but those are facts. And it is important to face up to these things. We shall not develop the right enthusiasm for such things, however, unless we fertilize our inner life by considering the great events of world history, seeing them in the right light—not that fabricated tale written in our handbooks and taught in our schools today, but the true history of the world that can be found by looking at things in the light of the spirit.

It is quite unthinkable for a present-day protestant Christian to consider that people once felt it to be true to say 'the god walked on the earth and the ruler was the god' and 'there is no kingdom on this earth where gods are still to be found, for the ways in which one is made a god are in the realm where the supersensible dwells, within the Mystery'. In the early times of Egyptian history, which in part was still prehistoric, the Mystery was indeed something supersensible. It was only when the mysteries were made into churches that the church became the symbol for the supersensible.

Present-day humanity has no wish to look to the points of origin of its historical development. It lives like someone who has reached the age of forty-five and has forgotten what life was like as a boy or a girl, at most remembering back as far as his or her twenty-fifth year. Try and visualize what it would mean for the inner soul life of someone of forty-five to remember nothing that happened before the age of twenty-five. Yet that is the state of mind humankind is in now, it is the state of mind in which the people arise who are to be the leaders of humanity. Out of this state of mind something is attempted that is to give the orientation for a social system. The most important thing is that human beings come to see humanity as a living organism with a memory that should not be trodden to death, a memory reaching back to things that still have their effect in the present day, and because of the way they do take effect, literally ask for something new to be poured into them.

We merely need to strike this note a few times and we shall see that there is need for something in the present time that makes all the empty words that are flashing up all around come to nothing. It would be good if a sufficiently large number of of people were to realize how serious the present situation is, and out of this realization were to arrive at something that is really new. The sad thing is that people today have been given great tasks and yet would most of all like to sleep through those tasks. The particular task given to the anthroposophical movement for decades now has basically been to shake humanity out of its sleep, to point out that humanity needs to be given something today that truly changes the present state of soul to the same extent as the dreamer's state of soul changes to being fully awake and alive for the day, when he wakes in the morning.

This I intend to be the conclusion to the two aspects of history seen in the light of spiritual science I discussed during my present stay in this city. If only something could emerge from our anthroposophical movement that would truly fire our social ideas, filling them with warmth and energy. Social impulses are needed in the present age, that is so obvious when we look at events that we really should not fail to see it. These social impulses can only come to fruition if a new spirit is poured into human evolution. This should be realized particularly by the people who from one side or another come to join the anthroposophical movement. On the soil of this anthroposophical movement truthfulness and alertness are necessary, real alertness. Modern civilized society has got into the habit of being asleep in public life. Today people are so much asleep one might fall into severe doubt on seeing the external course followed by people in the pursuit of their affairs—were it not for the fact that one stands within spiritual life and perceives the course taken by spiritual affairs behind the physical world. The external course people pursue in their events clearly spells it out that people fight shy of having any part in the search for truth in the phenomenal world. They are so glad they do not have to look at the events that are happening. You can see that when people are told of something happening somewhere today, they stand there on their two feet and give no indication of having heard something that is of profound significance for the way events will go. People hear of deeply significant things that must inevitably lead to ruin, to decline and fall, and they do not even feel indignation. Things are going on in the world, intentions are alive in German lands that should horrify people—yet they do not. Anyone incapable of being horrified at these things also lacks the power to develop a sense of truth.

It has to be pointed out that healthy indignation over things that are not healthy should be the source and origin of enthusiasm, of the new truths that are needed. It is actually less important to convey truths to people than it is to bring fiery energy into their lethargic nervous systems. Fiery energy is needed today, not mystical sleep. Longing for mystical peace and quiet is not of the essence today but rather dedication to the spirit. Union with the divine has to be actively sought today and not in mystical indolence and comfort.

This has to be pointed out. We must find a way of making it possible again for our minds to connect a divine principle with our outer reality. We shall only be able to do this if we consider without bias how people found their gods walking the earth in the earliest empires. We must find a way in which our human souls can walk in the spirit in spiritual worlds, that we may find gods again.

Stuttgart, 13 June 1920

One particular fact, a fact we have been discussing here a number of times, is causing concern to anyone wishing to work along the lines of a spiritual science in the spirit of anthroposophy. I am referring to the fact that modern humankind is basically failing to pay attention to the powers of decline that are clearly in evidence, to powers that must inevitably take our present civilization to the edge of the abyss if they are allowed to come into effect.

Surely we have to admit to ourselves that many things are coming up from the profound depths of human nature and coming to realization; or in other words that there is a great deal going on at present. On the other hand many of our fellow citizens simply cannot make up their minds to pay proper attention to what is really going on.

It is reasonable to say that at the present time little effort is made in cultural life to take a wider point of view and pay genuine attention to the forces that shape our world. There is one school—I have characterized it a number of times over the years—that has its roots mainly among the English-speaking peoples and is rather secretive about its work. It is however extraordinarily effective. A second school is the movement that has come together because people want to take account of the instincts of the masses, instincts that are understandable and indeed also justifiable. In its extremes this movement is represented by people who have no idea of human evolution, who know nothing of the principles that mean progress for the world. Certain conditions, however,—I shall refer to these later—enable them to hold a position of authority in spite of their narrow-minded views and in spite of a natural inclination for criminal activities that is in fact quite considerable. They are of course clever people and able to be to the fore in public life nowadays because they impress people.

The third movement that has an effect in cultural life is based on particularly energetic representatives of the different confessions—confessions of all kinds—who also know very well what they want. They are the fountainhead of everything that usually comes under the heading of Jesuitism. Many people talk about Jesuitism and the like, but still large numbers of our fellow citizens are little inclined to pay proper attention to what is really going on.

To get a proper idea of current events one would have to take account of a number of things. One thing to be particularly taken into account however is connected with a fact I also mentioned in my first public lecture here.[20] It is the fact that when it comes to their frame of mind, particularly as regards the way they form ideas, present-day people are in many, many instances continuing in a way that was only suitable for the forming of ideas during the Middle Ages. That was a great and significant way of thinking, but it is now out of date. Some people have gone very intensely into the medieval way of developing sensibilities and forming ideas. These are the people who hold more or less socialist views, and there are many of them all over the globe. The ideas current among them come to expression above all in a belief in authority that is almost limitless. They cringe before anything that assumes authority by simply taking a strong line among them. This has made it possible for people like Lenin and Trotsky[21] to impose their tyranny on millions of people with the help of just a few thousand. That particular movement is spreading from Eastern Europe into Asia at an incredible pace. It imposes a tyranny worse than anything seen during the worst periods of oriental tyranny.

All these things need to be considered in forming an opinion on current events. It has only been possible to give a rough outline. Basically the only opposition to these trends—and we are still thinking in terms of major forces in world history, forces shaping the world—comes from what should ideally be a truly honest, sincere and genuine spiritual-scientific movement. If we compare the interest brought to this spiritual-scientific movement with the interest those other movements have aroused within a relatively short time, and with the influence these movements have gained, we have to say that interest in this spiritual-scientific movement is as good as nil at the present time.

We do not fail to recognise of course that there are many people who go along with this spiritual-scientific movement, or at least tell themselves that they go along with it. There would be an enormous difference, however, if people really took note of the intensity with which those other three movements work for the things they want to bring to the fore, and then compared this with the intensity of interest that there is for spiritual science. The spiritual-scientific movement is really approached in a very superficial way, superficial in the way people feel about it. The other movements on the other hand are arousing a limitless intensity of feeling.

Does anyone clearly understand—making it the centre of both heart and mind—that if spiritual science is to intervene to any serious extent in the forces that shape the world, people must first of all give recognition and proper value to initiation knowledge, or initiation science as we call it? Initiation science today also needs humanity's firm and decided interest. Many people believe they are sincerely devoted to it, yet the interest they muster is still rather superficial, subject to all kinds of unimportant considerations.

The people I have often called the real big shots in the Anglo-American movement have initiation knowledge, but certainly not for the benefit of humankind. Everything based on Jesuitism has initiation knowledge and in its own peculiar way Leninism also has initiation knowledge. Leninism knows how to put things cleverly, using rational ideas produced in the head, and there is a definite reason for this. The cleverness of the human animal, the cleverness of human animal nature, is coming to the fore in human evolution through Leninism. Everything arising from human instincts, human selfishness, comes to interpretation in Leninism and Trotskyism in a form that on the surface seems very intelligent. The animal wants to work its way to the fore, to be the most intelligent of animals. All the ahrimanic powers that aim to exclude the human element, to exclude everything that is specifically human, and all the aptitudes that exist within the animal kingdom—I have often stressed this—are to become the forces that determine humanity.

Consider—and this is something else I have often stressed—the conceit shown by humans when they invented things such as linen paper, paper made from wood or the like; in short, paper of any kind. Well, wasps and similar creatures made this invention very much earlier, building their nests from the same materials as those from which we make paper. There you have human cleverness within animal nature. If you now take all the cleverness of this kind that exists within the whole animal kingdom, and imagine ahrimanic powers taking this up and making it come to life in human heads, in the heads of people who follow only their egotistical instincts, you can see that it may be true to say that Lenin, Trotsky and others are the tools of those ahrimanic powers. That is an ahrimanic initiation. It belongs to a different cosmic sphere than our own world does. It is however an initiation that also holds the potential for getting rid of human civilization on earth, getting rid of everything that has evolved by way of human civilization.

We are therefore dealing with three schools of initiation. Two are on the plane of human evolution and one is below that plane, though it is an initiation of tremendous will power, almost unlimited will power. The only thing that can bring order into all these developments, setting a goal that is worthy to be called human, is contained within genuine spiritual knowledge. A true goal and genuine sincerity will however only come from this spiritual science if it is made into something that involves the whole of our life, taking note how much empty chatter, how much conceit and inner egotism comes to expression in so much of what is usually said in its name. These things cannot be left unsaid. On the contrary, we need to discuss them over and over again. How else can we hope to give souls the power today that is needed to prevent civilization going into total decline.

Let me take a few minutes to give you a very concrete picture. Just a short time ago I read the following in a newspaper:

> Religion is a fantasy that arises in human heads as a reflexive response to the way they relate to each other and to nature. It is doomed to die a natural death in the triumphant progress of a clear, scientific and naturalistic interpretation of the truth that is evolving hand in hand with the planned evolution of a new society.[22]

Considering what one comes up against nowadays with regard to souls fast asleep in the present age, we may well ask ourselves how many people reading this kind of thing in a newspaper article pull up short as though stung by a viper, because a truly dreadful symptom comes to expression in those lines. People do not reflect on what would happen on this earth if these words came to realization:

Religion is a fantasy that arises in human heads as a reflexive response to the way they relate to each other and to nature. It is doomed to die a natural death in the triumphant progress of a clear, scientific and naturalistic interpretation of the truth that is evolving hand in hand with the planned evolution of a new society.

'Religion' does not refer here to some confession on other, nor to some religious movement that one may quite rightly consider to be wrong, nor merely to religion in the narrower sense, but to all that is moral. If the thoughts expressed in those lines were to come true the result would be that human society in every part of the globe would very rapidly become a herd of animals, animals capable of very sophisticated thought, however. If a way cannot be found now for opposition to arise against the principle that is growing in the East of Europe and spreading across into Asia at an incredible pace, civilization will be doomed. The ideals expressed in those lines would then become reality.

In the light of such impulses in world history I do not think it is justifiable for people in some places to wish to continue with the mystical small talk within closed circles, small talk that against my wishes has in the long run also come up in spiritual science working towards anthroposophy. Some people even consider it the ideal! I do not think it is right to continue with this in any form, totally disregarding what is demanded of us in the wider interest of humanity on this earth. It must be our will to consider those wider interests of humankind without bias. We must make an effort and become truly serious about certain basic principles—not merely in theory, using our intellect, but instinctively. Those principles have been obscured by all the confessions in Europe and America and the intention is to obscure them yet further.

We know about the virulent propaganda campaign being launched against spiritual science working towards anthroposophy, we hear the bullets whistling all around. If therefore opposition arises in some corner or another it would be a pity to give oneself up to the harmful illusion—an illusion indeed that today merits punishment—that we may ever hope to achieve anything by converting people who after all are the authorized agents of something or other that belongs to the past.

We cannot and must not be opportunists or go for compromise. That should be our special meditation every morning, as it were. There have been well-meaning people who have said we should simply try and explain to people in one direction or another how we are endeavouring to bring the Christ Mystery to the world. The more we do this, the more bullets whistle around our ears from certain quarters. Nothing goes more against the grain for instance with certain Catholic or Protestant groups today than that humankind should today gain true understanding of the Christ Mystery. It is not in their interest that the true Mystery of Christ comes to be known; all they want is to hold on to the old ideas. If we had some kind of strange and peculiar creed concerning Christ they would treat us as a harmless sect, as odd characters, and not fight us with the intensity we have come to experience. Within the two schools, quite apart from the third, there are however quite a number of people who know that our aim is to speak of the Christ Mystery out of the truth, and of social order out of the triune principle. This makes them sit up and listen; it makes them say: 'It would take the ground away from under our feet if we were to go for the truth; let us therefore vow to destroy it.' People do not fight us because we are in error, they fight us because it is realized in certain quarters that we want the truth. There is no point is saying anything else about some of the things that go on today. The cultural movement I am speaking of has a profound interest in absolute clarity, particularly also clarity of thought.

Remember some of the things I have told you. What is the essential point when we come to see what humankind needs above all else today? The essential point is that our powers of thought—everything we have by way of ability to form ideas, except for sensory powers—have come down to us from our life before birth or life before conception. Everything we human beings are able to think we have brought into the physical world when we were born; we have brought it with us from the life we had before we were born. All the thoughts we evolve whilst we are in our physical bodies are faculties that govern the whole of our essential human nature between our last death and the birth process that brought us into our present life on earth. When we are thinking here and now, the powers of thought we use, not the thoughts, are a shadow image of something that was at work before we were born or conceived.

Try and think of what we call the forces of nature today, of what goes on in lightning and thunder, in the movement of waves, in the way clouds are formed, in the rising and setting of the sun, in wind and rain, in the way the plants rise from the ground, in the way animals are conceived and born and grow. Think of all the natural processes you see all around; then think of them merely as a picture, not the reality. So, please, think of everything you have around you by way of natural forces casting its shadow somewhere or other, and of these shadows being taken up into a container and presenting themselves to us as pictures. The relationship that exists between nature as she actually is now and the reality that lies behind is similar to the relationship between life before birth and our faculties of thought in the present earth life. Just think that there you have everything that happens to your soul between death and rebirth—I am showing it in diagrammatic form—and then its shadow arises; a shadow arises of everything you have there and this shadow becomes the content of your head, the content of your thoughts; it is your faculty of thought. What you are thinking now, those are the forces active before you were born. That is 'nature' in the spiritual world, if I may put it in such a paradoxical way. The evolution of humankind cannot progress unless we become aware that when we are thinking, the existence we had before birth influences our faculties of thought. Having entered into my present earth life, I am continuing the life I had before birth when I am thinking.

Who puts up the greatest opposition to this idea? The greatest opposition is put up by religious confessions that maintain more or less the following: 'A human child is born. It pleases two people, a male and a female individual on this earth, to come together and God creates a soul in the spiritual world, a soul that then connects with what is created between two people in the act of begetting. That is how the human individual comes into being.' This is of course very different from what I have just been saying. It is what confessions live on in our modern civilized worlds. They all teach that when two people copulate the spirit very kindly creates a soul up above, a fresh new soul; it is then sent down to unite with the physical body which has been created, and something new has come into existence. To whom do these confessions address themselves? They address themselves to terribly egotistical individuals who simply cannot bear the thought of being extinguished when they die. Yet they are able to bear the thought—for they have got used to it over the centuries, indeed soon it will be millenia—that it pleases God to create souls for human beings procreated here on earth. What their egotism does not allow them to accept is the thought that death puts an end to it all.

Of course you all know what life after death is like. I do not need to go into it here. But let us turn our attention to something quite different. Preachers in their pulpits always need to assume that they are speaking to people who cannot bear the thought of death being the end of it all. The water they have to pour down from their pulpits—irrespective of the particular creed followed by the people who sit there below them—must make it clear to them—I mean unclear, of course—what happens after death. They have to choose words most liable to excite the egotism of people; they have to utter phrases that are fully in accord with the egotism in the souls of people.

Let us think what would happen for instance—to give a particular example—if someone were freely and in all seriousness to make certain aspects of the Roman Catholic confession his target, say the dogma that when two people copulate it must please God to send a freshly made soul down to them. What would happen if criticism were to be aimed at this? Someone going into the whole issue without prejudice would find that it has nothing whatsoever to do with anything to be found in the true Christian faith. They would find that during the Middle Ages the teachings of Aristotle infiltrated theology and that Aristotle represented these ideas on the basis of misunderstood Platonic ideas, saying that a fresh soul is created for every newly generated human body and unites with it. Something taken for granted as a fundamental tenet in Christian beliefs in fact has nothing to do with Christianity but is an Aristotelian principle.[23]

Let us move on to something else. One element in religious beliefs is the dogma of eternal punishment in hell. Again, entirely an Aristotelian thought. Aristotle assumed that once a soul had been created, lived on earth and then come into the spiritual world, there was nothing it could do in the spiritual world, as he saw it, but look back for all eternity on what it had done during its one and only life on earth. Aristotle imagined that a fresh soul was created for every child, that this soul lived on earth until the individual died and then for all eternity occupied itself with the contemplation of what had happened during one life on earth. If someone had committed murder, they would have to look back on this for ever. That is where the dogma of eternal punishment in hell originated. It is a purely Aristotelian concept.

Just think, if the truth were to become known, instead of Aristotelian thoughts presented as Christian dogma, the people wishing to represent such Aristotelian ideas masquerading as Christian dogma would be scared out of their wits that people might find out about this, that people might find out that their priests were not teaching Christian ideas from their pulpits, but Aristotelian ideas that had crept into Christian teachings.

Christian beliefs also contain an infinite number of ideas deriving from gnostic teachings. The Roman Catholic sacrifice of the Mass has infinitely much in it that derives from the Egyptian Mysteries. Many of the rites of the Catholic Church—and the Protestant, too, in many respects—contain things the origin of which must be sought in all kinds of oriental religions. All they are after is that people do not find out where these things come from. What do they feel compelled to do? They have to resort to slander! They have to say that the people who are presenting the truth today are plagiarists borrowing from oriental and gnostic teachings and so on. 'Traubism' is the order of the day. They come up with learned calumnies like those presented by the clergyman Professor Traub[24] and all the people who parrot him. Why do people do such things? Because the truth is coming to light and they all have an interest in not letting it come to light. People will go on saying that what we are doing is taken from some source or other. They will provoke something that makes people go against gnosis and things that are part of the very fibre of their souls because they do not want it to come to light in its true form. Gnosis—one is supposed to say—is something terrible, something dreadful. Then people will ignore it, being afraid of it, and the preachers can talk about things that in fact have their origin in gnosis. It is the preachers who talk about things that originally came from gnosis, not the people who speak about what has grown in the soil of spiritual science working towards anthroposophy. What they are most afraid of is that there is such a thing as pre-existence of the soul, a life of the soul before birth and also conception, that the soul has its roots in the spiritual world through all the ages that any kind of knowledge and creed among humankind might cover. For if the truth were to become known there would be no room any more for such blasphemy as that the gods are obliged to send a newly made soul from the spiritual world for every single human body, so that they might unite. All these things have their origin of course in a desire for power that is getting very strong. Behind it all are thoughts of power. It is possible to put tremendous energies into such thoughts of power simply by following certain precepts.

What is going on in Dornach at the moment, for instance? All around, almost everywhere in Switzerland, articles on anthroposophy are being published not one sentence of which is true.[25] The whole campaign started when an article appeared that contained twenty-three lies. For weeks now, article on article has picked up on those twenty-three lies; they have appeared almost everywhere in the Catholic press in Switzerland and not a single sentence is true. Why is this happening? It happens because the many followers of these people are brought to a certain state of mind by being told untruths, a state of mind where it is no longer possible to tell the difference between truth and falsehood.

Think of all the efforts we go to in spiritual science working towards anthroposophy to form sufficiently clear ideas; for instance, as to how far the things we become aware of in human minds, in the form of dreams, may or may not be reflecting the truth. As human beings we cannot immediately distinguish truth from falsehood when something appears in the course of a dream. The same state of mind arises for a congregation when they are told lies by people who know that those lies will be believed. The soul is brought to a state, a mood, by those lies where it becomes the willing tool of those desiring power. It is easiest to get people into your power by planting illusions in their unsuspecting minds. Articles full of lies are systematically put out with the intention of creating the kind of mood that can be created with lies. That will be the inevitable consequence of the probabilism which the Jesuits have been teaching for a long time. It is merely a final consequence.

It is of course difficult to rouse modern souls from their general torpor to stand up against such people. The day before I left we were forced to arrange for a lecture—for we must fight, of course, even if we do not want to, against the lies that come up in Dornach. Dr Boos, one of the most courageous of our young protagonists, called on everyone who had anything to say on the subject of the lecture to join in the discussion—it was a public lecture, of course. When no one came forward he said openly and publicly that he publicly declared the cleric who had first written those twenty-three lies, a priest called Arnet in Reinach, to be unworthy of his priestly calling, for disseminating scurrilous lies.

One cannot help oneself. And then, even when this had been said, only one individual stood up among those present, a teacher, shaking in his boots if I may put it like that, and said: 'Just wait. There are more articles to come, and in the end you will see!' Well, all I could say was that there had been twenty-three lies to begin with, and the truth about those twenty-three lies will without doubt never emerge, however long it takes until there is an end to the matter even if the end does not come until the end of the world. Not the least attempt has been made in everything published so far—and a respectable number of articles have already appeared—to go into those twenty-three lies.

Other things have been tried, using a strange logic. The pamphlet by the Tuebingen speaker was brought into play—it actually played a large role—but the people who bring professor Traub's pamphlet into play in their articles have not properly understood what he said. They will write that this man Steiner is borrowing from all kinds of ancient writings, from the Upanishads, the Egyptian Isis Mysteries and the 'Akaskic Records'—well, I suppose the typesetter may have put that in, but on the other hand the clerical gentleman may have done so. I therefore said that it was not really my concern to correct printers' errors, but that it surely is a strange way of reading Traub's pamphlet if immediately afterwards the reader has forgotten that not even Traub says anything so stupid as that the Akashic Records are to be found on library shelves; I said that one cannot really accuse people of borrowing from that old tome, the Akashic records, for spiritual science based in anthroposophy.

Our attackers have also gained support among liberal thinkers. Dr Boos was going great guns in a liberal paper, saying that this was a deliberate untruth, since the writer must have known that there were no Akaskic Records in his library. He could not possibly have them in his library and so he ought to have known; he must have written a deliberate untruth. What did the person concerned do? He wrote that Dr Boos was evading the issue, as it was self-evident that the typesetter must have been responsible for the 'Akashic Records' error and not he himself. In his view the kind of sophistry that made authors responsible for that kind of printing error merely showed what kind of stable people came from.

Well, you see the kind of mentality one is dealing with. But do not underestimate it! You have to realize that it is going to be a hard fight, particularly in this direction. The aim is to prevent people from finding out about what I have been saying. What I said, first of all in the medical course, is the following: It is particularly when one is making serious efforts to determine the spiritual laws of this world, doing so on the basis of present-day life, when one tries to reach the deeper secrets of human nature by making these things one's own on the basis of present-day life, and then also finds them written in ancient works—albeit arising from an intellectual life that was more instinctive and atavistic—that one feels very humble in perceiving the greatness of the instinctive, atavistic intellect that human beings once possessed; that has been lost and must now be found again. These words were spoken in awareness of the fact that knowledge which today has to be sought within life was once instinctive wisdom given to humankind. Much of that ancient wisdom has of course survived in the religious beliefs, though it has become corrupted. Yet the people professing those beliefs want to make humankind fear that original wisdom, and when they talk about it say more or less the following: 'Those dreadful people who pursue anthroposophy today are borrowing everything from that ancient wisdom'. If they went into the matter they would find that the spiritual science offered to humankind in anthroposophy is very different from anything ever borrowed from anywhere, from the Upanishads or whatever. So we had to borrow indeed from that ancient tome called the Akashic Records! To prevent people getting sight of something that belongs to the present age our enemies are letting their bullets come whistling from all around.

Let us be clear about one thing. You may feel tempted now and then to stress the good points of one thing or another. The alliance between Jesuitism and the Social Democrats which is getting closer and closer by the day is something entirely natural. There is nothing unnatural about it. The Social Democrats are equipped with the same kind of ideas as the Jesuits, only they take them the other way round. One thing, however, that differs from all else that is felt is the 'eternal nature of the human being'. This has become the teaching of egotism. It is restored to its true form when the pre-existence concept, of a human soul having a life before birth, or before conception, once again becomes the effective moral principle. The knives will come out to fight this idea. We shall only be able to progress in the world if in the first place truth has inner power. This inner power can only be effective, however, if in the second place people have the courage, however few they may be in number, to carry this truth in their souls, carry it in their souls in all seriousness, uprightness and honesty and without compromise. It is useless for us to play down the tremendous difference which exists between true Christianity and the Catholic and Protestant Aristotelianism which holds the idea that souls are created for bodies as they arise through procreation. We must not play down this difference. If we do play it down we will not even notice where the idea of power, the desire for power, has its real origins.

I find myself referring again and again to the pastoral issued by a Roman Catholic bishop.[13] This document really exists. According to it the faithful must regard their priest as ranking higher than God and Christ, for each time the priest performs the consecration at the altar Christ is forced to be present by that altar, to be present in the bread and the wine which is His body and His blood. The priest therefore has greater power in the universe than a god. That is what it says in a pastoral that really exists and has also been quoted in many other pastorals. Now you may ask me if that is consistent with the abolition of the spirit by the Council of Constantinople[26] in 869. The answer is yes. A Roman Catholic saying that God is more powerful than a priest would say so because people will not accept any other view nowadays. People are so much asleep in their souls that they never ask themselves: 'What was the person [27] writing to Moleschott really saying who had the nerve to say that a criminal, a liar, a murderer is a moral person only if he can be fully himself and is an immoral person if he does not bring to expression what he has in him, for this would impose restraints on his individuality, and that an inclination to murder is just as valid as other inclinations are'? Modern souls do not have the courage to say to themselves: 'If scientists continue to teach the kind of basic philosophy that they have been teaching, the inevitable conclusion simply has to be that criminals, murderers, are just as good as someone trying to act morally, as it were. People merely lack the courage to admit this.' When materialism had its flowering, at the time when people like Vogt, Moleschott and Buechner[28], all of them courageous men, were publishing their writings, such things were admitted. The present age is too cowardly, however, to make such admissions. Nor is there sufficient courage in the sleeping souls of the present to admit to oneself: 'If you go by the spirit of those creeds and statements a priest is indeed more powerful than a god.'

The school of thought represented by spiritual science working in the spirit of anthroposophy must above all work towards clear thinking in every respect. Its message cannot be grasped if thoughts are unclear, it cannot be grasped in a vague and vaporous mysticism but only with crystal clear thoughts, thoughts which in my *Philosophy of Freedom*[29] I have tried to show are the starting point for genuine human freedom.

We may continue our discussion of the subject when I am able to speak to you again. I hope this will be soon.

Stuttgart, 24 June 1920

Today's meeting provides a further opportunity for me to speak to you who are friends of the anthroposophical movement before I leave. I wish to do something which in a way is particularly close to my heart, to discuss some of the things that really need to be discussed. It is possible that most of what I have to say today is a repetition of things that have been discussed on a number of occasions from all kinds of different aspects, things now also taken into consideration in public lectures. There are reasons, however, why it is necessary for us to consider some of them once again today.

I have often stressed that it is necessary for a sufficient number of people to fully understand the following. To prevent the decline into which we have got ourselves in the civilized world from continuing into utter ruin, certain impulses must be brought into modern civilization that can only arise if spiritual science reveals the nature of the world to its fullest extent.

Materialism has come to Europe over the last three or four centuries, coming to a crest in the 19th and then tumbling over in the 20th century. It has a peculiarity that seems paradoxical, particularly if one fails to realize the true causes. The peculiar thing about materialism is that it has no possibility of recognizing the material world as it really is. I think I have already given you an example of this. The materialistic way of thinking has in more recent times given rise to an idea that is believed by a great many people, namely that the heart is a kind of pump in the human organism that pumps the blood through the organism. This idea of the human heart being a pump comes up in all kinds of variations nowadays. The facts are rather different, however, and should be seen like this: The whole of our rhythmical circulatory system is something alive. It cannot be compared with a system of channels or the like with water flowing through them, water kept circulating with the aid of a pump. Our rhythmical circulatory system, our blood system, is something alive. It is kept alive by a number of factors, the major factors being breathing, hunger, thirst and so on. These clearly function at the level of soul and spirit. Our blood system is set in motion by entirely primary causes, and the movement of the heart arises when this spiritual principle enters into the rhythm of the blood. The rhythm of the blood is the primary, living principle, and the heart is caught up in this rhythm. The facts are therefore entirely the opposite of what every professor of physiology is teaching today, with the result that it is dinned into people's heads at school and indeed from their earliest childhood.

It therefore has to be said that materialism has not even managed to get a real understanding of the physical processes relating to the heart in the human organism. The material aspect in particular is completely misunderstood. This is just one of many examples. Material things in particular have found no explanation whatsoever under the influence of materialism. The heart is not a pump. It it something we might regard more as a sense organ incorporated within the human organism to give human individuals a kind of subconscious perception of their circulation, just as the eye perceives colour in the world outside. Basically the heart is a sense organ within the circulatory system, yet exactly the opposite is taught nowadays.

This would appear to be an example of limited relevance. I can imagine some philistine saying: 'Well, it can't do much harm if people have entirely the wrong idea about the nature of the human heart. Of course, if doctors had the wrong idea about the nature of the human heart that would be cause for general alarm. After all, it does make quite a difference in human life if doctors have the right or the wrong idea about the heart.' But this also holds true for other things. Everything is connected with everything else in life, and because of this humankind is absolutely full of wrong ideas, completely upside-down ideas. One might well think, if one was serious about it, that being hung up on wrong ideas would cause real havoc in our thinking processes. It certainly does. Our thinking is utterly ruined because it has been dinned into us and we have become used to thinking that things are the opposite of what they really are. That is why we never acquire the habit of steady, purposeful thinking. How can our thinking grow purposeful in social life, for example, if in areas where truth should be sought above all else we are in fact going in the opposite direction?

You see, some things that are important to know are a closed book for people today. When the human organism is investigated in conventional institutes nowadays, in physiological and biological laboratories, in hospitals and similar institutions, the brain for instance is examined by analyzing it bit by bit as it presents itself to the eye. The liver is examined by the same kind of analysis. In doing so, people never consider one thing that is absolutely essential if one wishes to understand the human being: The whole of the head organization as we have it today and everthing it governs is entirely different from the rest of the human organism.

Let me show you what lies behind this. You can draw it like this. I intend to lead up gradually to what I really want to say. You can say that the human being has two organs of perception, and the direction in which they perceive is approximately like this [see (a) in the diagram]. Two other directions in which we perceive show a certain relationship to these. In diagrammatic form I would draw them like this (b):

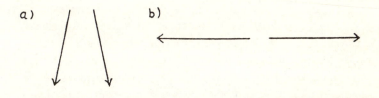

The human being thus perceives in four directions, as shown in the diagram.

I deliberately did not tell you where these organs are to be found in the human organism. If I draw nothing but two arrows to indicate direction (a) here, where one stretches out, as it were, to perceive, and two others here, (b), where we perceive sideways, it makes no difference at all if these are the directions in which feeling and sensation pass through my legs and these where they pass through my arms. Here we have something that is in accord. I perceive my own gravity, as it were, I stand with my two feet on the ground. I really perceive something. And I also perceive something when I stretch out my hand, stretch out my arm, even if I do not actually touch anything. I can draw it like this (a). The same drawing can also stand for something different. Imagine this is the horizontal plane. The two arrows could represent the two visual axes; I could draw the two visual axes like this. And these arrows (b) could indicate the directions of my ears. The same diagram would serve to indicate perception by the eyes and ears. On the one occasion I have the whole organism within the head, though the plane has turned through a 90° angle, on the other within the rest of the organism. There is a higher point of view where both are the same. Our two legs are merely directions in which we perceive that have become flesh. The same directions exist in a less physical form where they extend from the brain through the eyes to perceive colour. Elsewhere we perceive gravity and everything connected with it. We see our weight and we step on colour, we could say, if we were to change the two things over, entirely in organic terms, of course. I hear the blackboard chalk, I touch a C or C sharp that is sounding. The difference is merely one of degree. In the head everything has gone through a 90° angle and is less physical; the other is in the vertical plane, and is physical. In the final instance both are the same. It is only that I am aware of the way my eyes step on colours, my ears touch sounds; I know about it, it is part of my ordinary conscious life. Everything my legs see with regard to gravity and all kinds of other things that my arms hear—all these are in the subconscious sphere. Conditions belonging to the cosmic sphere are present in the subconscious. With the whole of my subconscious I have knowledge of the cosmic sphere, knowledge of the way the earth relates to other bodies in the universe, knowledge of the universal background to gravity. I hear the music of the spheres with my arms and not with my ears.

Thus we may say that we have a lower organism, as it is called, with subconscious cosmic awareness, and we have a head with earthly awareness; this however is a 'conscious' awareness. The whole of the human being is organized on the basis of these differences. Our outer form and configuration depends entirely on these differences. You know that the head we carry today is the transformed body of our previous incarnation, our previous earth life, and that the rest of our present organism will be the head in our next life. The head, then, is the rest of the organism which has undergone a transformation. It is more perfect, more finished in a way. As a result the legs have become fine visual threads extending beyond the eye and stepping on the colours in a very lively way. The arms of our former life have become so ethereal that they now extend from our ears and touch the sounds we hear.

These are concrete facts about the human being. It does not get people anywhere to know about repeated earth lives and so on. Those after all are dogmas and it makes no difference if you have the dogmas of the Catholic or Protestant church or the dogma of repeated earth lives. Real thinking only starts when you enter into concrete events, when you come to realize that looking at the human head you are looking at the transformed body of your previous earth life, and that the head you had then was the transformed body of the preceding life—you must imagine it without the head, of course. The head you see now is the transformed organism of the last life lived on earth. The rest of the organism as you see it now will be the head in the next life. Then the arms will have metamorphosed and become ears, and the legs will have become eyes. We must look at the physical world and understand it in its transformed non-physical form, our intellect must illumine the material world in this way. Then at last we shall have what humankind is much in need of today. Once the human mind has been organized so that it no longer produces the kind of folly that has been put forward as a potential social theory, particularly in the second half of the 19th century, human beings will indeed be ready to develop social ideas that can be put into effect in this world. It is necessary to gain a thorough understanding of this today. It is a serious matter when people say today: Something else will have to take the place of the science which has evolved and is so highly respected, of all the things that are generally disseminated. There can be no other way.

It is nonsense, and I also said so recently in a public lecture,[30] to talk about setting up adult education thinking that the same kind of work can be done there as at ordinary universities. It is the work done at the universities that has brought us to these disastrous situations, because it has become the materialistic view of a few leading personalities. This is now to be presented to the masses; that is, millions are to head for the disasters that so far have come about because the wrong lead was given by a few. Something that proved useless for a few is now to be spread among many. It is not as easy as that, however. Popular education cannot be introduced simply by teaching outside the universities what until now has been alive inside them. It would mean teaching something that is altogether unsuitable for human beings. This may sound radical, but it is absolutely essential that it is fully understood if there is to be even the least hope of the decline being halted and something new and positive developing.

These are the things one wishes one could speak of in words that truly go to the heart. These concrete truths must reach as many hearts as possible. It was therefore important to me to point out in my public lectures that something has been achieved in the Waldorf School, that anthroposophy has positively influenced the history lessons in some places. I was also able to refer to the teaching of anthropology in class 5. There, too, anthroposophy was effective. Not that one would teach anthroposophy to the children—we would never think of doing such a thing—but lessons come to life if anthroposophy is the foundation, if the inspiration of anthroposophy is there in what we teach. This brings the souls of the children to life; they are quite different when this influence is there. It would be taking the easy way simply to teach anthroposophy in our schools. No, that is not what we are about, but rather to use anthroposophy to enliven the subject matter. It will of course be necessary for anthroposophy to come alive in oneself first of all, and that is something that really comes hard, to let anthroposophy come alive in human beings. Otherwise the potential is there today for all kinds of disciplines, not only in science but all kinds of disciplines in life, to have the full benefit of what life in anthroposophy is able to give.

That is a general way of looking at it. Let me go on to something specific, so that you can see the things we are considering in their proper context.

Marxist philosophy, Marxist views are widespread today. They have their most radical expression in Leninism and Trotskyism, which are destroying the world. A view of history known as 'historical materialism' plays a great role in Marxist philosophy, particularly the dogma of the fundamental importance of the modes and relations of production. Millions of proletarians have accepted this dogma according to which tradition, law, science, religion and so on are like smoke, like an ideology rising from the modes and relations of production—you will find further details in my book *Towards Social Renewal*[31]—and that the modes and relations of production are the only reality on which to base one's view of history.

It was very important to me on past occasions—this has to do with the feeling I have that I was really able to achieve something and create a potential basis at the Worker's Education Institute in Berlin[32]—to speak in proletarian circles about the view that the modes and relations of production are the only effective element, and to present a clear picture. My aim therefore was not to teach historical materialism but the truth. That was of course also the reason why I was thrown out, for it offended those in charge at the time just as much as the idea of a threefold social order offends people today. Authoritarian thinking and belief in authority were and still are as great in the socialist movement as in the Catholic church.

What really matters is to gain a clear understanding of social relations in this world. Real understanding of the natural threefold order of the human organism, of the way the human organism is an organism of nerves and senses, rhythmical organism and a metabolic organism, as shown in my book *Von Seelenrätseln*,[33] leads to a way of thinking that can also apply to social life. People of little understanding will say: 'You are using analogy in applying the threefold order of the human body to the social organism'. This is nonsense of course. Anology is not the method used in *Towards Social Renewal*. All I said was that if people succeeded in letting their thinking escape from the strait-jacket put on it by modern scholarship and particularly public opinion, they would free their thinking to the extent that it will be possible to think sensible thoughts concerning social issues. The kind of thinking that puts the human brain side by side with the liver, examining everything as though it were of the same substance, will never come to sensible conclusions.

Using external analogies we might say: The social organism is threefold by nature and so is the human organism. The head is the organ of mind and intellect; it should therefore be compared with the cultural and intellectual life in the threefold organism. The rythmical system establishes harmony between different functions in the action of the heart, in respiration—that would be the rights sphere in the social organism. Metabolism, the most physical, material aspect—someting mystics tend to look down on to some extent, though they say they also have to eat and drink—would be compared to the sphere of economics.

This is definitely not the case, however. I have repeatedly pointed out on other occasions that in reality things are very different than mere analogy would make them to be. It cannot be said, for instance, that summer is comparable to the waking state for the earth and winter to a state of sleep. The reality is different. In summer the earth is asleep, in winter it is awake. I have gone into this in detail.

The same applies if we consider the real situation in comparing the social and the human organism. The economic sphere of the social organism actually compares to the activities of the human head. As to the sphere of rights, the legal sphere, people were quite rightly comparing this, the middle realm, with rhythmical activities in the human organism. The life of mind and intellect however has to be compared with the metabolism. This means that economic life has to be compared with the organs that serve the mind and intellect, and the cultural and intellectual sphere of the social organism with the metabolic organs. There is no way round this. Economic life is the head of the social organism; cultural life is the stomach, liver and spleen of the social organism but not of the individual human being. It is of course too much of an effort for anyone whose thinking is in a strait-jacket to make distinction between social life and the life of an individual person.

Again the essential point is that spiritual science prepares us to see things as they really are and not to produce analogies and elaborate symbolism. We will then arrive at important conclusions. We shall find, for example, that we can say: But in that case economic life, if it really is the head in the social organism, will have to live on the rest of the organism, just as the head does in the human organism. In that case we cannot say morality, religious life and the search for knowledge are ideological elements arising from economic life. Quite the contrary, in fact. Economic life is dependent on cultural life, on the metabolism of the social organism, just as the human head depends on respiration, on stomach, liver and spleen. We then come to see that economic life arises out of cultural and religious life. If we did not have a stomach we could not have a head. Of course we also could not have a stomach if we did not have a head, but it is the head after all that is fed by the stomach, and in the same way economic life is fed by cultural life and not the other way round. The socialist theories that now threaten to spread through the whole of the civilized world are therefore quite erroneous, a dreadful superstition. No one has thought to look for the truth in recent centuries; on a purely emotional basis everyone has been promulgating the kind of truth their class and point of view suggested to them. Now at last it is realized that it is a total delusion to see historical evolution as the product of the modes and relations of production. The idea is now to compare the actual facts and not to talk in analogies. Now a realistic view is taken and it is realized that if the stomach is undermined in the human organism, the head will suffer. In the same way there can be no sound metabolism in the social organism and economic life must fall into decline if morality, religious life and intelligent thought are undermined in the social organism. Nothing in fact depends on economic life; primarily everything depends on the views, the ideas, the cultural life of humankind.

The head is always dying—I have spoken of this in other lectures—and we only maintain the head organism because it is constantly dying and the rest of the organism rebels against this. The same applies in the sphere of economics. Economic life is constantly bringing death and decay into the progress of history; rather than generating everything else it brings about the death of everything. This element of death constantly has to be counterbalanced by what the cultural organism is able to produce. The situation is therefore exactly the other way round. Anyone speaking in materialistic terms and saying economic life is the basis for progress is not speaking the truth. The truth is that economic life is the basis of something that is always dying in stages, and the mind and spirit have to make up for this dying process. To proceed the way people are now proceeding in Russia is to help the world to its death. The only possible outcome of proceeding in this way is to help the world to its death, for the simple reason that the laws of death are inherent in the things that are being done there.

You can see the eminent social importance of these things. We have now been working in anthroposophy for twenty years, and all the time I have tried to make it utterly clear and apparent in all kinds of lectures that what matters to us is not the cultivation of a philosophy full of inner self-gratification, a kind of spiritual snobbery, but to develop the most important impulse that is needed in the present age.

I wanted to present this to you again today in a slightly different form in connection with a number of things that can help us understand the essential nature of the human being. It is important that those who call themselves friends of the anthroposophical movement clearly perceive the connection between this anthroposophical movement and other events as we know them.

The ideas put forward by myself and other friends are often seriously distorted. It is therefore difficult to speak freely to such a large audience, even if it is anthroposophical. As there is no immediate opportunity, however, to discuss these things at a more intimate level and yet it is necessary to speak of them, let me draw your attention to a few things. We must be aware, particularly here in Stuttgart, that the anthroposophical movement we have now had for twenty years has indeed reached a new stage. If we are serious about the movement this means we have accepted the obligation to follow this change, to adapt to this change. You must properly understand that because our friends Molt, Kuehn, Unger, Leinhas[34] and others have attempted to take the anthroposophical approach to its practical conclusion something has happened that concerns us all. It concerns us all and we must take account of it in everything we say and do. The fact is—and let us be very clear about this—that until then the anthroposophical movement was a current in the life of the mind and spirit. Such things continue on their way, cliques and closed groups, however objectionable, that go by personal and heaven knows what other interests, may form; a spiritual movement may even proceed by the agency of privy councillors like Max Seiling[35]. One does of course have to approach it properly in view of what is called for, but for as long as it is a purely spiritual or cultural movement it can be ignored. Now, however, three things have grown out of this spiritual movement.

The first followed the appeal I made last year.[36] It now forms part of the struggling threefold movement, the Association for a Threefold Social Organism. This has not yet been able to get anywhere near the real objectives. What the appeal had to say has in a sense met with rejection, and it would be a good thing to be fully aware that there has been this rejection, that only very little of what was intended has come to fruition.

This does of course mean that I have many requests made to me. The idea has come up in Dornach, for example, of issuing a further appeal that would make it known internationally what Dornach means to the world. I had to explain to our friends that in the ordinary life outside that is now heading for a breakdown, appeal usually follows appeal, programme on programme. We cannot do this if we work out of anthroposophy. It is important to realize that, in a way, it is not at all healthy if something is undertaken that does not come off. It is important to make a careful assessment of the chances of success, and not just do what comes to mind but only the things that have a chance of success. This is why I then said—it is important and I must ask you to consider it carefully—that I would not dream of making a similar appeal again, for what has happened to the first appeal should not happen a second time. It was possible to let the appeal for a Cultural Council[37] go out, for that was not my work, but we must be very clear that things are getting a great deal more serious than people are inclined to think if something like the anthroposophical movement stands behind them.

Three things have now evolved out of the anthroposophical movement, in a way, each of them quite distinct. A threefold order following that appeal—we will have to work at it, for it partly meets with rejection; secondly the Waldorf School;[38] thirdly the financial, commerical and industrial enterprise called *Der Kommende Tag* (Dawn of Tomorrow).[39]

Coming to Stuttgart in the past, when we only had the anthroposophical movement—I am referring only to Stuttgart—I would spend three or four days here and you know how many personal interviews I managed. These things have had some effect, as is now becoming apparent. It was not without significance that whatever had happened in the meantime—people will understand what I mean if they want to—could be put to rights again in those personal interviews. Events could then proceed until the next time. Now the position is such that following those outer developments one has to attend meetings from morning till night, and indeed well into the night, and there is no question of continuing in the ways we got used to when we were only an anthroposophical movement. Now there are many people who feel that it is a nuisance that things are no longer the way they were. It is necessary, however, to look at all the changes and really say to oneself: Things have changed since the spring of last year and this will have to be taken into account.

The situation cannot remain as it is, but a united effort must be made to see that it does not remain this way. It cannot remain as it is because everything that is done—be it for the Waldorf School or the *Kommende Tag*—has its basis in spiritual work. Without the spiritual work that has been done and must continue to be done there is no point to it all. The spiritual work must give form, vigour and content to the whole. To continue the way we are going would mean that the institutions which have now been established would swallow up the original spiritual movement. We would be taking away the original basis. Nothing growing out of the anthroposophical movement should be allowed to swallow up the movement as such.

You see, these are serious matters we have to discuss today, and I think at least some of you will understand what I mean. Things will not be different unless we accept it as a reality that anthroposophical work has been done for many years, for decades. This work must be seen as something real.

I would ask you also to consider the following. There is much conflict in the world, but where is most of this conflict to be found? It takes a certain form and people fail to notice, but most of it takes place in the sphere of spiritual endeavour. There is no end to the conflict within the body we call the anthroposophical movement, for example. When our movement evolved out of older practices—it was necessary to start from these, you know the reasons—that is, when many people familiar with the old theosophical practices joined our movement, I had the feeling that a gentleman, who at the time was particularly vehement in his defence of the line we were following, would very soon be in conflict with various other people. Conflict is likely to be particularly bad in this sphere. In fact I always made it quite clear that the gentleman in question, a theosophist of the purest water, would not only come in conflict with others, but that his right side and his left would be involved in a desperate struggle. People will find that the left side of this individual will have the most dreadful quarrel with his right side.

It will of course be necessary to develop the other extreme, where the conflicts that constantly arise are overcome. Such conflicts are dut to the very nature of spiritual movements, because they all aim to develop the human individuality. The other pole, the other extreme, of human understanding, must be there as well; it is the pole of human understanding where it is possible to enter into a human individual, to go deeply into the life impulses of another person, and so on. It must be possible for the *Kommende Tag* and the Waldorf School we are now running to be given a sound moral basis by the anthroposophical movement here in Stuttgart, the moral basis that is the work of decades, or at least should have been such. That has to be the foundation, for it is the only way in which we can go ahead and restore the balance between a life consisting of meetings and the necessary spiritual work which after all should be the basis. We cannot achieve this, of course, if things go on all the time where one is told, for instance, that dreadful things have been going on again, with someone causing trouble all the time, someone upsetting all the rest. Well, that may be so. To date—and on this visit such things have come up again countless times—I have not been able, however, to pursue such an affair to the point where the second person, when approached, told the same story as the first. When it came to the fifth or sixth person, I would hear the absolute opposite of what the first had told me. I do not want to criticize, to apportion praise or blame, really, not even the latter, but that is how it is. What is needed, particularly among anthroposophists, and I have said this on many occasions, is an absolute and unerring feeling for the truth. It is very difficult to continue working in all these areas unless there is a basis of truth, of genuine, immediate truth. If there is this basis of genuine truth, surely it must happen that when something comes up and one pursues the matter further a fifth or sixth person would still present the same facts. Yet it happens that I am told about something 'dreadful' and everybody I ask tells me something different. I cannot, of course, apply the things I have from other sources to external life; I have said this many times. It is not a question of whether I know about it, know who is right and who is wrong. The question is whether the first says the same as the sixth or seventh. What I know has nothing to do with it. As a rule I do not allow people to pull the wool over my eyes, and that is not why I ask people. The reasons are quite different. As a rule it does not interest me very much what people tell me. The point is that I hear what the first person says and then the seventh, only to find on many occasions that one person says one thing and the seventh says the opposite. It evidently follows that one of the two things cannot be true. It seems to me that this does follow.

In outer physical life which for this very reason is going into a decline people have always wanted to shut their eyes to the function, the crucial significance, of untruths. Even unintentional untruths are destructive in their effects. In spiritual science working towards anthroposophy it is absolutely essential to realize that <u>an untruth in the life of mind and spirit is the same as a devastating bomb in physical life</u>. It is a devastating force, an instrument of destruction, and this in very real terms. It would certainly be possible to do important and fruitful work in the spiritual sphere again, in spite of the many new developments, providing these things are given some attention—<u>objective attention</u>, however, not subjective attention.

You know I do not normally go in for tirades; it is not my habit to moralize. Just for once, however, I really must discuss the facts that have become very obvious at this time, because the situation is serious. We are looking at undertakings that must not fail, that will have to succeed, and there can be no question of any kind of failure; we have to say today that they shall suceed. They must not however swallow up the original anthroposophical movement, and this means that everybody must do his share to ensure that the moral foundation established in the work of many years really exists. Everybody must do his part. It is really necessary for everybody to to their part.

It saddens my heart that I am unable to respond to almost all the many requests that are made to me. I had to keep refusing to help my friends because time cannot be used twice, and meetings go on not only from morning till night, but even well into the night. Quite obviously I cannot use the same time to talk to individuals. The membership in the widest sense must come to its senses and get rid of the things that play a role in all aspects of life here, the kind of thing I have just been mentioning. Every single member must reflect and see that here in this very place these things have to be done away with. Unless this is done—and these things are connected—it will not be possible to find the time to do real fundamental spiritual work. Everything arising out of anthroposophy will succeed. Yet unless some things change the original spiritual movement will be swallowed up. The will impulses of those who consider themselves the bearers of this spiritual movement would then lead to a new materialism, as the original spiritual movement will have been aborted. The spirit needs to be nurtured or it will die. Materialism does not arise of its own accord; you cannot create materialism, just as you cannot create a corpse. A corpse is produced when the soul leaves the organism. In the same way everything created here on a spiritual basis, out of something that has soul, will become entirely material unless there is a genuine desire to nurture the spirit. It means that above all the moral and ethical basis which we have been able to establish is given careful attention. It is necessary above all to ensure that we do not become subject to illusion, that we do not think it is enough to accept certain views just because they are easy to accept. We must look at life without flinching.

It is really very bad for people to say things like: 'The threefold order is a good thing; we must take it up.' Feeling rather good about it they will say: 'I am getting something organized and it is very much in accord with the threefold order; aren't I good! It makes me really feel good getting something organized that is a nucleus of threefoldness'. Licking your lips morally speaking, full of inner self-gratification—you may feel like this when you are doing such things, but it does not mean that you have a sense of reality. The threefold idea is true to reality because it requires genuine effort to bring it to realization. Many people's ideas are however so unrealistic that the idea of threefoldness goes against the grain with them. The first and most essential thing is for this idea to be taken up by a sufficiently large number of people. We must have the necessary sense of reality and practical common sense.

Eight days ago I had to speak here in Stuttgart about the consequences the threefold order has for the management of landed property.[40] I said that the threefold order obviously aims to achieve a situation where social exchange, social conditions relating to landed property, are such that land cannot be bought and sold like other goods. That is entirely based on reality; to say the opposite would be unrealistic. I had to discuss the subject on a day when I actually got here late because we had been going round the countryside all day trying to buy land. If we have a sense of reality we cannot base ourselves on the threefold order and say: 'I must be good; I am forming a nucleus for the threefold order.' No, it has to be accepted, and there can be no illusions, that in a certain respect the only possible way in which we can work for a threefold order is by working on the most important aspect, not basing our work on the immediate present.

It is not a question of morally licking our lips as we say that we follow a particular idea. This would make it unfruitful and abstract. It is a question of really seeing the reality, seeing what is necessary. This is the difference between people whose approach is utopian and dogmatic and those who take a practical view. The latter will take an idea as far as it can go, but they are not unworldly people living for some private pleasure; they take hold of the reality. We really only give ourselves up to illusion for our own private pleasure. This must be realized. It is also necessary to realize that many other things go in the same direction. I am sorry, it could not be helped. There were quite a number of things that I could have talked about on this last occasion before my departure. I might have drawn your attention to many things that were put to me more or less in passing, things that do have an effect on the fruitful activities. One of the main problems with those fruitful activities is that there is a constant need to have endless discussions on matters that should be dealt with in half an hour, because things are thrown into the pool that really should not be there. If you have sound thinking habits—and those are the habits we must acquire if spiritual science as it is presented here is to come about—and then find yourself—I am not speaking theoretically—right in the middle of what is nowadays called business practice, the best way of defining what goes on is that people kill as much time as possible, that time is wasted. There are practical people today who boast of being busy all day long. If they did not waste so much time, their work, which let us say takes ten hours, could be easily done in one hour. Time is killed particularly in what is called active life today. This killing of time causes thoughts to be drawn out. Entering into practical life as it goes on today one really gets the feeling that one is in a noodle factory where thoughts that ought to be concentrated are drawn out, pulled apart like strudel or noodle dough; everything is pulled well apart. It is dreadful to come across those spread-apart thoughts that are cultivated in practical life. If you wanted to use thoughts like these to get a clear understanding of the world, of the things I have spoken of today by way of an introduction, you would not get anywhere. All this 'strudel-dough thinking' has arisen in the process of killing time. Thoughts that ought to be concentrated, for that is the only way for them to be effective, simply come to nothing by being drawn out. Something which functions properly at a certain density will of course be useless once it has become thin and worn. Many of the things that play a large role in modern economics are quite useless when it comes to making world affairs progress. Our particular task would thus be to grow concise in our thinking also with regard to practical things, and not to kill time. However, time still has to be killed these days, unless the anthroposophical movement, which after all supports our enterprises, becomes what it ought to be: A movement based on truth in every respect, a movement where all untruth eliminates itself because we have no use for it and because it would immediately show itself to be what it is.

This is what I wanted to say to you today. It is not addressed to anyone in particular. Please do not continue to go around saying that I was aiming at one thing or another in particular. I wanted to give you a clear picture of the facts as they are in general. The world situation is serious today and the things that have been going on among us here in Stuttgart really reflect the serious situation that exists for the whole of civilization. The things that haunt us in our community here can teach us a lot about the things that haunt the world as a whole.

I do not wish to hurt anyone's feelings. Nor do I want to moralize, to preach at you. The intention has been to discuss the things that have been obvious to the eye and to the soul on so many occasions over the last two weeks.

Stuttgart, 25 July 1920

There has been a basic theme to everything we have been considering here in recent times. Again and again the point has been made that when any work is undertaken or any proposal made in connection with the anthroposophical movement proper regard must be paid to the gravity of the present situation. In principle everything I have said so far has been in accord with that basic theme. It should also help more and more of our members to come to feel this in their souls. We will continue along these lines. Today I want above all to refer to something that can help us to find the right inner attitude, as it were, to the spiritual-scientific movement that has anthroposophy for its goal.

There has now been scientific evidence that Western culture is in a decline—you know about the book by Oswald Spengler [41]. How do people regard the search for truth within this culture, irrespective of the degree to which they even admit to this? People who imagine they have both feet firmly on the ground, considering themselves to be eminently practical people, regard the search for the truth as something theoretical and not as a real deed accomplished by the soul. It is essential for us today to come to the realization that the search for truth is a deed accomplished by the human soul. We must come to realize that when we gain insight this is no mere theory, no individual point of view, but an actual deed infused with will impulses, a deed in the total context of the evolution of the earth and of humankind.

To begin with let me use a more methodological approach to show the way recognition of the truth must be seen as a deed, using a fact from cultural history as an example. I have frequently spoken of two streams going in opposite directions in the life of the human soul. One of these is the abstract mystical stream, the other the abstract materialistic stream. The latter has developed with the evolution of science over the last three or four centuries. Basically it has entered into all areas that play a role today in the progress of human evolution.

The traditional religious creeds hardly play a role in the real progress of human evolution the way they are presented nowadays. They could however play a role in furthering the decline of Western culture.

It if were a matter, for instance, of bringing Spengler's idea of the decline of the West to full realization, the traditional religious faiths officially represented by the Jesuits, by positive Protestantism and so on, would be able to do their part. They would be of no account, however, for progressive evolution. As I have said on a number of occasions, the materialistic stream is clearly in evidence even in people who themselves are quite unaware of this. Characteristically, and it is something we must keep in mind, even the theosophical school was affected by materialism in certain areas when it went by the title 'theosophical school'. The descriptions given of the human etheric and astral bodies in those circles, where these bodies were merely said to be more subtle forms of matter, with people imagining some kind of mist or cloud, surely were nothing more or less than materialism in spiritual guise. Spiritism is of course materialism most heavily disguised as something spiritual, for it speaks of the spirit when in fact its aims are merely to prove the material existence of the spirit, to present it in material form. Materialism has eaten its way into everything spread about by way of popular literature, above all in popular books and journals where people are informed as to what is 'true'; it is present in everything that is spread about like this, irrespective of whether it comes from Catholic or Protestant sources. This materialism on the one hand relates to the progress made in culture. It must be taken into account and taken positively into consideration. Traditional historical elements like the religious confessions must of course attack anything that is new; they must fight intensely against anything that is new. This, however, does not have to be taken into serious account when we form our ideas of the present, for it goes in the direction of decline. Materialism on the other hand produces the very things we ought to know about in the present time, though they are of course presented in a materialistic way, in materialistic interpretation. If we wish to share in the work that brings progress in cultural and intellectual life we must know what materialistic anatomy, materialistic physiology, materialistic biology and the sociology of the present age have brought to light. We must be fully informed about these things and out of this very knowledge gain the power to transform materialistic knowledge, the materialistic way of thinking, into spiritual knowledge. It is therefore of definite value in the present time to give full consideration to what materialism has to offer. We cannot transform, say, the Catholic philosophy of the Middle Ages the way some people imagine. This can only be transformed with the aid of Thomism, as I have shown in Dornach,[42] though it then transforms itself. Materialism can be metamorphosed into an inner spiritual life. Anthroposophists therefore have no reason at all to despise the things that materialism has to give. We have to reckon with materialism. Anthroposophy cannot be evolved out of a blue haze, it must be evolved by people who are alive in and part of modern life, a life that in the first instance is a materialistic one.

The moment we wish to see materialism in the light of the true progress of humankind we must develop a particular basic feeling, the very feeling that many people of the present age, and above all academics of the present age, do not have. This is the feeling that everything immediately around us in the world we perceive with the senses, everything our eyes see, our ears hear and so on, is not real and that we should not look for reality in that direction. We must develop the feeling that it is utterly mistaken to look for atoms and molecules in the world we perceive around us and to consider them to be real, or even commemorative coin. Some scientists are particularly proud to say that they do not take atoms and molecules to be real but use them as ideograms, ideal points in space. It is immaterial, however, if you assume atoms to be physical or ideal points. What matters is whether you take a living comprehension of spiritual entities as your starting point or whether you consider the idea of such living comprehension an abomination and base yourself entirely on what may be gained in the material world. This applies also to atoms seen as points where forces are located. As soon as you base yourself on atomistic ideas you find yourself in a materialism that must lead to doom. We can only deal properly with the world we perceive through the senses if we treat it as a phenomenon, as a form of manifestation. Matter is not even present in the things we perceive through the senses. We must therefore develop the feeling—we can do this thanks to the findings reported in the anthroposophical literature—that when we use our eyes and look out at the whole starry firmament, the cloud formations, the contents of the three kingdoms (mineral, plant and animal) and also the fourth kingdom, the human kingdom, we must not look for anything material in the things that come to us through sensory perception. Matter is not behind any of them! All we perceive are phenomena like the phenomenon of the rainbow, for example, though they may appear more solid than a rainbow. No one should consider a rainbow to have some kind of outer reality—like a solid bridge with its span in seven colours—but see it only as a phenomenon. In the same way we should regard all the things we encounter through our senses as phenomena, however solid they may appear. A rock crystal can of course be taken hold of, whilst in the case of the rainbow we could not take hold of anything. Yet although it may affect our sense of touch, it should still be called a phenomenon. We must not allow our fantasy to create some kind of physical reality, in spite of the view of nature that is generally taken today, a view that is following the wrong path. The 'physical' phenomena we come across therefore are definitely not material phenomena, are not the reality of matter. They are mere phenomena; they come and go out of another reality that we cannot comprehend unless we are able to conceive of it in the spirit. That is the feeling we must evolve—not to look for matter in the outer world.

The real goal of anthroposophical development is missed above all by people who despise outer materiality, people who say: 'The things we perceive in an outer way are mere matter; we must rise above such things!' That is quite wrong. The things we perceive outside are not material, we cannot look to them to find the world of matter. We simply do not find matter in the world that impresses itself on the senses. You will come to see this if you read what our anthroposophical literature has to say, and take it in the right spirit.

You then need to develop this feeling further. Here we come to aspects that people find highly uncomfortable today because they come very close to the experience we know can be had with the Guardian of the Threshold. They are uncomfortable; yet unless we enter into them we will make no progress in inner development. We have to go through inevitable discomfort if we are to get from theory to reality. The search for truth must be based on facts. Anyone who thinks matter can be found in the world which we call the material world—the world we preceive with the senses—is mistaken, and the error involves more than mere theory. There are people who think that because others say it is 'matter' it really is matter; this kind of word-cleverness is in vogue nowadays. If anyone thinks it is enough just to say: 'It is wrong to look for matter in the world we perceive with the senses', they cannot be said to be speaking out of spiritual science working towards anthroposophy. Spiritual science does not consist in correcting other people's theories. Spiritual science must make the search for truth a deed. It must be a search for knowledge based on strong will impulses, that is, it must enter into the facts even where it merely makes definitions or explains things. And this is where the situation gets uncomfortable.

It is easy to say to someone that they are wrong in thinking that matter is to be found within the outside world, which we perceive with the senses, and to tell them to change their views. That is just talking theory. To accept theories, to oppose theories, to correct them—all that is theoretical talk. Spiritual science cannot in all reality be satisfied with this. The essential thing is to develop our sensibilities to a point where we perceive that someone caught up in materialistic views of the material world has a thoroughly unhealthy organism. We must progress from purely logical definition to a definition that takes hold of realities, in this case the constitution of the human individual. We must become convinced that it is not merely wrong logic to say that matter is to be found in the world we perceive with the senses, but that anyone who considers that what his senses perceive is physical substance is truly on the road to constitutional feeblemindedness. We must perceive that it is sickness to be materialistic in that sense.

We want our ideas to take hold of reality. We cannot do so whilst we continue to think in theories. Everybody supposes that they only need to have good instruction to change their views. Spiritual science always demands that we are alive as we develop and that we restore ourselves to health where we have been materialistic in the above sense, since a departure from the right way means sickness, the road to feeblemindedness.

At this point things come very close to the insights to be gained in meeting the Guardian of the Threshold. When we encounter the Guardian of the Threshold and thus enter into worlds other than the physical world—worlds that add something new to the physical world—all theory comes to an end, the intellectual mists clear and reality begins, with every word saturated with reality. Then we can no longer say that someone is expressing correct or incorrect views. We have to say that they express their views out of a sick or a healthy mind. Then we encounter reality. Nor can we say that someone should correct their views. Instead we must say: 'If you are on the road to sickness, to feeblemindedness, you must change course and develop a strong, healthy mind again.' You see it is not enough to correct the so-called philosophies that spread their mists about. For anyone wishing to become a spiritual scientist it is essential to go through a change that is a very real process, and not to be satisfied with something that is intellectual, logical or theoretical. The gravity of the present situation is such that the pathological nature of an intellectual view of the world must be vividly apparent to us.

An attempt has been made to outline one particular aspect, to characterize in the light of reality the materialistic aspect of our cultural life today. The other aspect, the polar opposite of this, is the mystical approach. Mysticism is the refuge of many people who are dissatisfied with materialism. They find that materialism is not right and therefore feel they must follow a different philosophy, a different path in their search for truth than the paths followed by materialism. People then try to develop by following an inner path and to find the spirit along that path. I have frequently spoken of mysticism as a spiritual stream that has the same right to exist in its one-sidedness as materialism has, providing one perceives this one-sidedness. I have spoken of mysticism as a kind of reaction against the materialism which has developed in the American and European civilizations over the last centuries. I have referred to this a number of times, also in the pamphlet published during the war that was also sent to the men at the front.[43] This mystical stream must be considered in more detail, again without any of the theorizing that is so common. When it comes to mysticism, people think that by withdrawing from outer life and entering deeply into their inner life they will find the spark of which Meister Eckhart spoke.[44] They think they will come upon the revelation of the true spirit that cannot be found in the outer material world. Mystics do however tend to be real materialists. Taking the opposite route, mystics mostly are harsh people and out-and-out materialists. They start to shout as soon as the material world is mentioned, considering themselves superior to such things—as has often been said, they feel they are above such things. The point however is that we must not merely theorize but go into the reality. The point is that we must look for the reality behind those mystical endeavours. It is important to realize what comes to life in us when we become mystics, what is active in us when we become mystics. You can find out about it from the anthroposophical literature. We have to say that this is the very soil where physical matter is to be found. We find materiality active in us when we become mystics. Consider even the most sublime mystic—what is he bringing into play in his soul? He brings into play things that boil and bubble in his metabolism, however refined and subtle this metabolism may be. Matter as such is to be found within the human skin, and not in the outside world that impresses us through the senses. We come upon physical matter when we allow things ignited in the metabolism to arise within us. Look at the way Meister Eckhart spoke of God with such depth and conviction. He actually told how he had scrupulously brought to awareness what was bubbling and boiling in his metabolism. It seemed to him to work towards the central heart and there to become transformed into something that could be perceived as a spark of the divine self in the human being. That is the small flame metabolism ignites in the heart.

The true nature of physical matter is thus found by following the path of mysticism. The genuine fruits of Goetheanism must be raised to a higher philosophy of life. In the same way we must clearly understand that the fruits of mysticism must be considered to gain an interpretation of activity in the material sphere. We do not discover material processes in our chemical laboratories. When a chemist is at work in the laboratory, the processes taking place in the retort are external phenomena, just as a rainbow is an external phenomenon. That, too, is phenomenon and has no real materiality to it. We learn about real materiality when we see the bubbling and boiling of the processes that go on inside our skin ignite the way a stearin candle ignites to burn with a flame. That is where materiality has to be sought, and we only see mysticism in its right light when we realize that all the inner experiences mysticism provides in its one-sidedness are material effects; true materiality is to be sought in there. We must not look for physical matter by analyzing chemical processes. We must look for physical matter in every organic form that goes through its complex chemism and physiology inside the human skin. Mysticism gives us the solution to the riddle of physical matter. Mysticism however *only* gives us the solution to the riddle of physical matter. We must not reinterpret the inner materiality of the human organism to the effect, for instance, that when we see a burning candle we say: 'That cannot be the fruit of something inherent in the candle. There is a tiny spirit inside that candle and this spirit produces the flame.' That would be nonsense of course. It is also nonsense to look for the reality of the spirit in the experiences of a mystic.

It is necessary to arrive at a very definite idea, even if this is difficult. This is a threshold truth. We do not get far with what can be achieved in mysticism, for there we are dealing with phenomena that are like opiates, we are given up to our egotistical desires that allow themselves to be defined as anything but the materialistic aspects of our own inner processes. The bewildering multitude of phenomena surrounding us in the world of the senses does not allow us to go so far as to realize that in fact none of it has any materiality. Let us consider what we are actually seeing when we look at a distant planet, say, or a fixed star out there in space. What are we actually seeing? We do not see the green plant cover of the ground, the cloud formations, brown or grey earth and so on that we see around us on this earth. The stars and even the moon are too far distant for that. Everything that lives out there on those alien heavenly bodies has an inner aspect, has material processes that have been transformed. What we see through the telescope are the material processes active in the highest form of existence on the star in question. In the same way, if that other star, let us say the moon, were to look at us through a telescope, would it see our plants, animals and so on? No, the earth is far too far away for that. Pointing a telescope at the earth the moon would be looking into your stomachs, hearts and so on. That is the content which shines forth into the cosmos. The human kingdom is the highest on earth and because of this someone looking from outside would see what goes on inside human skins. When these things which are visible to distant stars become ignited in our own inner awareness they are the things mystics experience.

So you see that anyone seriously devoted to the anthroposophical view will have to penetrate this second, equally uncomfortable threshold truth that it is mysticism which teaches us what matter is on earth. We cannot know anything about even the simplest of earthly forces if we merely look at the outside world. Just open a book on physics. You know it discusses gravitation, earthly gravity. It always includes the comment, however, that it is impossible to know the true nature of gravity. People are in fact rather pleased with themselves when they explain that the essential nature of gravity is not known.

How can we get to know the nature of the force that makes the chalk fall down when I let go of it? The force called gravity can be understood as follows. At a certain point in life, perhaps after the thirtieth year or even earlier—it depends on how kindly destiny deals with us—we can make a discovery when we observe ourselves in the light of spiritual science, rather than by the usual methods of observation. The methods of spiritual science do to some extent introduce us to the methods of genuine self-observation. About the thirty-second year, therefore, we can make a discovery. Observing ourselves not in the abstract way of mystics but genuinely, we shall achieve genuine self-observation; for instance by noting that living from the thirty-fifth to the fortieth year, say, we have changed at the organic level. Some will note that their hair has turned grey; it also happens nowadays that men grow bald. We find we have changed. Unless however we have gained the ability to observe ourselves we shall have no experience of these changes, we shall not have inward experience of what happens with these changes. The experience can be gained if people apply to themselves what it says in my book *Knowledge of the Higher Worlds*.[45] From about the thirty-second year onwards we have the experience that the body has to be carried differently, that it becomes heavier. That is our inward experience of gravity, of gravitation. It has to be experienced inwardly.

None of the wishy-washy things talked about in mysticism are as important as a concrete fact like this, the inner experience of growing heavier. You cannot gain this experience if some person stands here and lets a stone drop from his hand. You do not observe the gravitational pull by watching a stone drop, for stones have no real materiality. You must observe yourself, this time looking not into space but into time, that is, the way you experience things before and after. We must progress from experience in space to experience in time. Things never to be found in the world of the senses must be gained through inward experience. They are the second element belonging to reality.

Experiencing the outer world of the senses we have truth but no knowledge. Experiencing inwardly in a abstract mystical way we have merely knowledge and no truth, for we are under an illusion concerning the basic phenomenon of inner life; inward experience being the flickering flames of material processes. Anyone looking for materiality in the outside world is interpreting the world in an ahrimanic way. Someone else may merely look for truth in an abstract way within himself; he or she is interpreting the world in a luciferic way. Genuine spiritual science in the light of anthroposophy holds the balance between the two, with truth and knowledge interweaving. We must look for truth at one extreme and knowledge at the other and become aware that living realities become polar opposites when knowledge is brought into truth and truth into knowledge. Then the search for truth becomes a real deed. Then something is happening. We are not merely producing logical definitions or correcting our views, but something is happening when human beings endeavour to gain inner experience of knowledge and look for the truth outside them, endeavouring also to let each enter into the other.

This has to be understood in the present age. The present age must understand that human beings must hold the balance between the two extremes, between the ahrimanic and the luciferic poles. People always tend to go in one direction. In the Trinity Group in Dornach[46] the luciferic element is above and the ahrimanic below. The Christ is in the middle, holding the balance. These things can be presented as ideas, can be made into the essence of ideas. They then become truth and knowledge. It is also possible to represent them in art, but then we have to forget about mere ideas and seek to find them—in line, in form, in configuration. Then it becomes the Trinity Group in Dornach, for instance. The whole is of the spirit, however.

Mysticism is one-sided and so is materialism. We must know that the two have to be interwoven and we must be alive in our doing, knowing that the true inwardness of the human being is to be found in being alive in one's doing. Our age wants to be one-sided and embrace materialism and this means that it is indeed on the road to feeblemindedness. I have shown that we must not be content with theories but must know in truth and reality that materialism shows itself to be what it is—a road to feeblemindedness—as soon as we meet the Guardian of the Threshold. We must aim for a state of health, and not merely disprove things in order to arrive at something else. The opposite extreme is abstract mysticism. We should be able to develop the feeling that in reality it is the road to infantilism—to put it bluntly, to childishness—a condition appropriate only for small infants. A child as yet untouched by the world, living entirely in physical materiality, in the processes of its physical organs, is exactly the type of the mystic, though the mystic will have the same experiences at a later stage than a child. They will of course feel different, those experiences, but an infant also experiences this concentration of organic activity in the heart. Sensing this concentration it will kick its legs in the air and wave its arms about and we can see how this peripheral activity is the opposite to the concentration of activity in the heart. If people remain childish all their lives, if they are too lazy to take in the things that only materialism can give, they reject outer materiality; it means nothing to them, they see it as something low that must be overcome. And then they kick their legs in the air and in doing so produce their mysticism. That is the threshold truth, the unpalatable threshold truth. Everything that is abstract and mystical, inducing a feeling of self-gratification when people concern themselves with mysticism nowadays, with things that make them lick their lips when they appear in print, though in reality they are the equivalent of kicking one's legs in the air in one's thoughts—all that is infantile. It has to be clearly understood that whereas materialism leads to feeblemindedness, abstract mysticism leads to infantilism, to childishness. True life is found when we find the balance, the equilibrium, between materialism and mysticism.

Again it is rather difficult to do this, and things really get uncomfortable. When you want to balance the scales you must not despise anything that is present in excess on one side and upsetting the balance. You must really try to put into both scales what is needed to maintain equilibrium. In the same way you should not despise anything that takes you into the sphere of matter, saying to yourself that it will cause feeblemindedness. Quite the contrary: anyone wishing to enter into things must step boldly into reality, saying to himself: 'I will have to follow the path that would lead to feeblemindedness if I were one-sided in my pursuit; but I am armed against it. I am also armed against remaining one-sidedly on the other path; I retain what is necessary from childhood days but do not remain a child.' That is how the balance must be sought between materialism and mysticism. That is a true sense of life. The sense of life holds the balance between feeblemindedness and childishness. Anyone who cannot be bothered to see these things clearly will not be able to enter into reality. People only grow feebleminded if they fail to note that normal people have to overcome feeblemindedness day by day, hour by hour. Feeblemindedness is a constant threat and we only remain human by remaining childish, i.e. inspired. Anyone holding on to childishness in the right measure is a genius. We are geniuses only to the extent to which we have held on to childishness into our thirties; but this childishness must be properly counterbalanced. Thus we have to say that we are all in danger—how shall I put it—of becoming geniuses or remaining childish infants. It could go one way or the other.

As soon as we come close to threshold truths, our ordinary ways of expressing ourselves no longer work; things that normally are quite separate blend into each other at this point. All words acquire a different meaning, and we might say—it would be quite amusing to represent this in a painting or sculpture—'Here is the threshold of the spiritual world, with one individual on one side and one on the other; one is active in the spiritual sphere, the other in the material world, and they are yelling at each other. The one who is in the spiritual world yells: "Childishness!" The other yells across from the material world "Sheer genius!" ' Just as a tree looks different when seen from another point of view so things look different depending on whether we look at them from the spiritual point of view or out of materialism. From the spiritual point of view the genius of someone who has retained the ways of a child, forming ideas in play, has to be called childishness, we must see it as childishness when we are on the spiritual side. Childishness is regarded in a different way from that point of view. There we know that human beings descend from the spiritual world, that they come to live in a physical body; we see that a child is still lacking in skills, is still undeveloped, but we also see the most sublime spirituality alive in that child.

It has caused considerable annoyance to some people—that numskull Dessoir,[47] for example—that in a small work I published. *Spiritual Guidance of Man and Humanity*,[48] I have shown that the wisdom involved in giving shape and form to the brain of a child is far greater than the wisdom human individuals are able to produce in later life. Numskulls like Dessoir cannot grasp this. For them, the full range of wisdom is what they write in their books. The thing is, however, that when we say 'childishness' from the spiritual point of view we perceive how the human spirit has descended as a ray of the divine spirit, and that it was fully developed when it did so. It entered into a human body that was still undeveloped, taking hold of it, working it, with the result that after just a few months the brain has become something different, and the whole body is something different in the seventh and fourteenth year of life, and so on. Childishness is not a term of abuse, therefore, for childishness is seen to be the descent of the spirit into the physical world, a first taking hold of the body, a stage where one is still a child, still in a human condition where the head has not yet been cleared of the spirit. That will happen as the rest of the body develops, for this develops fastest, whilst the head contains far more spirit. That is the image we have when we speak of childishness from the spiritual point of view. The head of a child is full of spirit and—this is an unpalatable truth—as we get older the spirit gets less and less, our heads become more and more petrified. A child still has a great deal of the spirit. This gradually evaporates. I may be permitted to use the term 'evaporate' in the sense that the spirit evaporates from the head down into the rest of the organism. So you see I am speaking of something most sublime when I speak of childishness as it is seen from beyond the threshold. If I speak of childishness from the earthly point of view it means that one has failed to progress. The language of the earth and that of heaven are different, alas, and it is part of the tragedy of our age that people do not even want to understand the language of heaven. Since it has become customary to speak in the most earthly terms possible from the pulpit it is no longer possible for people to understand the language of heaven.

It then can easily happen, when one has something to say within a certain context—expressing it out of that context, of course, and having prepared the way before saying the words that come from beyond the threshold, words to the effect that the entities of the spiritual world evaporate downwards—that the following may occur. Let me present a picture to you of something that really happened. It may happen, then, that someone writes: 'Steiner says things evaporate in a downward and not an upward direction.' Some professor of anatomy[49] gets hold of this and reads it out to an audience which he himself has prepared by asking them to bring children's trumpets and rattles when someone is going to talk about genuine anthroposophy. So a lecture on anthroposophy is given. Then the professor has the word and reads out something like this, having somehow got hold of it, and the students use the trumpets and rattles they have brought along to produce the kind of scientific argument that has become customary in those circles. This is something that really happened in Goettingen the other day. Have a look at the supplement to the recent issue of our Threefold Order journal. [50] You will find it there.

These are serious times in which we live and on Friday I want to continue in the vein in which I started today, when I characterized the true face of materialism for you on the one side and that of mysticism on the other. I will then show you what we are called on to do. We are not called today to gather in sectarian groups, but to come alive and intervene in what goes on in life, bringing anthroposophical impulses into the world of the present cultural life. If we understand what the present age asks of us we cannot remain one-sided materialists or mystics, we must take the road to reality. I have tried to characterize this in the pamphlet. Mr Molt took the trouble to put into print for the men at the front, so that they might learn something of the anthroposophical spirit. We must always keep in mind that these are serious times in which we live and that we shall only feel able to cope if we are open to the approach of something that properly speaking cannot even be given a name, using the old forms of speech, but imposes the necessity to find new forms of speech if the truth of our age is to be found. The search for knowledge must go beyond mere rumination, it must become an active deed. Then humankind will not slither into the doom of the Western world, for we shall find the upward path again. As long as materialism continues to use the symbols of childishness—those trumpets and rattles—to rebut anthroposophy, and mysticism makes use of materialism, dressing up utterly material processes as something spiritual, we shall slither into the doom of the Western world at full tilt. It is not a question of ruminating but of really doing something.

Stuttgart, 30 July 1920

Today I shall have to continue with some of the topics I discussed the last time I was here. It is particularly important, indeed necessary, to stress the connection between what I have said before and what I wish to add today. I have explained that the road to spiritual science calls for recognition to be given to two facts. One fact is that it is impossible to imagine that matter, physical substance, can be found in the outer world of our human environment. This can be clearly understood on the basis of many different things that can be learned through spiritual science. Our eyes behold the outside world, our ears hear the outside world, and we come to understand nature in a way when we use the intellect to combine the things we see, hear and perceive with the other senses. We then think we know something about outer nature. Yet we are in error if we think and believe some form of science will help us to find physical matter and the laws pertaining to it in that outer nature. Materialism was in error not because it was speaking of physical matter but because materialists thought they could find physical matter and the laws of physical matter, its infrastructure and essential nature, in the outside world. People saying they do not want to know about the outside world because it is a material world, and that they want to follow the inner mystical path to a world of the spirit, are therefore materialists just as much as people who simply interpret the outside world in materialistic terms. Their search along the path of mysticism shows that in their view, too, physical matter is to be found in the outside world. The people of more recent times are in error when they look for the essential nature of matter in the outside world. To put things right essentially means that we must no longer look for the nature of matter in the outside world and be very clear in our minds that however far we extend our sensory perceptions we shall never discover the nature of matter and its infrastructure, its laws. It has to be understood that all that exists in the outside world is Maya. It is the world of phenomena. Look as we may we shall never find anything material in that outside world.

On the other hand we must grasp a second, quite different fact. It is that the nature of matter, which materialism is erroneously looking for in the outside world, may be found within ourselves. We shall find it particularly if we become one-sided, abstract mystics. The contents of a certain mysticism coming to our awareness—experiences we think we are having—are nothing but the flame, I would say, that is lit within us by processes involving our physical organs. Considering the mysticism of Tauler and of Meister Eckhart, one is right in thinking that these men had a special faculty for experiencing these things and interpreting the physical matter in their bodies when the flame of awareness was ignited. They found the material world through mysticism. Until we know that external observation reveals only the world of phenomena, Maya, and that inward observation reveals only physical matter and its flame, we cannot get a clear, true picture of the nature of the world and the way human beings relate to this world. Physical matter is not to be found by applying science to the outside world, it must be sought within us, through mysticism. There we shall find its laws. The essential nature of gravity is not to be found with the aid of Atwood's machine.[51] Instead we can try—in our thirty-second year, or perhaps at another time in our lives—to become inwardly aware of gravity, so that we know from inner experience what it really means to experience gravity. Concrete inner experience should show us that between the thirtieth and fortieth year we grow heavier and heavier inside. We can gain inner experience of a property of matter that merely comes to expression in mystical experiences. I have tried to demonstrate the essential point by saying that anyone finding himself in the midst of the chaos of the planet, the way modern scientists do, cannot get a clear idea concerning these things. We see the plants, the animals, the cloud cover; we see the glittering light of the stars, we see rivers, hills and valleys and so on. Yet if someone were to observe the earth from Mars, for instance, none of these would matter. An inhabitant of the planet Mars observing the earth through some instrument or other—we may well imagine, and it would be in accord with the truth, though in a different way, that those who inhabit Mars have the kind of organization that enables them to observe the earth—would perceive nothing of the cloud formations, rivers and mountains we see, nothing of the phenomena relating to the mineral, plant and animal kingdoms. He would only preceive what goes on inside the skin of the human beings living on earth. Everything else would vanish before the eye of an inhabitant of Mars. He would perceive only what goes on inwardly in the organic life of human beings and for him that would be the material world of the earth. When we grow aware of a mystical element within us it is not what many mystics think it is but the flame that is cooked inside us. That is the place where we can find out about the physical matter of the earth. This form of self-perception takes us into the sphere of matter and of energy, an area where the people of the Western world have arrived at exactly the opposite view over the last centuries.

This gives an indication of the extent to which we have to change our thinking if the decline is to become an upward movement again. People think they are materialists or idealists or spiritualists because they follow a particular philosophy. That is not the case. We are far from being spiritualists when we say we contemplate the inner and not the outer life. It could indeed happen that someone is concentrating on his inner life and exactly by doing so comes to observe matter; the way it turns into a flame inside us. To find the right path it will be necessary to grasp what I mean, and to do so with the right inner attitude. The outer world as we perceive it with the senses offers only phenomena; it does not reveal the root and origin of the phenomena. Their root and origin lies inside our own skins. Anything we see outside should be regarded in the same way as we regard a rainbow. Anyone who believes a rainbow to be more than merely a phenomenon, thinking it to be something material spanning the heavens, is taking the wrong view. In the same way we are in error if, due to the fact that our sense of touch is also involved when we perceive the world around us, we believe we are surrounded by material things and not mere phenomena. The only difference compared to a rainbow is that other senses are also involved. Materiality cannot be found there, however, just as it does not exist in a rainbow. Everything outside us is phenomenon. The root and origin of the phenomena therefore is inside the human skin. The processes that carry the affairs of the earth from one age to another take place inside the human skin.

It may seem highly improbable and paradoxical to modern minds but it is nevertheless true that the phenomena which surround us today, and the laws apparent in these phenomena, are not the outer consequence of material events that occurred three thousand years before the Mystery of Golgotha. They are the consequence of what went on inside the bodies of Egyptians, of Chaldeans and others three thousand years before the Mystery of Golgotha. Those inner events have become outer ones. The outside world of those times has vanished, disappeared. Human bodies hold the germ for a future that may be reckoned in thousands of years. It is possible to see this by considering the natural phenomena of today, drawing a conclusion that may be bold but nevertheless revealing. People talk about the properties of the element radium. To someone able to perceive the reality of the spirit this sometimes sounds like children talking about something adult minds have long since come to understand on the basis of different facts. Modern physicists know that the radium which existed on the earth's surface up to AD 140 has since disappeared and no longer is radium. The radium that is found today has only formed since AD 140. Physicists are actually teaching this now. These things present themselves to human minds to force them, as it were, finally to give up the erroneous ways of thinking which had to be pursued for centuries for the sake of human freedom.

All this shows that it is necessary to consider the things spiritual science working towards anthroposophy presents to human minds in a totally different way from the way we usually look at things. It is necessary to abandon mere theory and consider the reality: to progress at all levels from abstract intellectual knowledge to active perceptiveness, to doing things, really doing something in relation to the world. As I have said before—but it is essential to make this point with real forcefulness—people think that some are materialists nowadays and others are spiritualists. A spiritualist will say: 'He's a materialist and has to be opposed because it is not true that the soul is the product of physical matter. What the materialist says is wrong and we have done enough when we have refuted his arguments. The materialist is in error and therefore must be opposed.' That is not the point, however. It is not a question of logic, of theories. Yet people always think spiritual science is all theory. Spiritual science working towards anthroposophy always bases itself on reality, sometimes of course seeking it in the place where it is to be truly found: in the true realm of the spirit. People who look to the outside world and seek to find matter everywhere by the methods now used in molecular and atomic theory—it makes no difference if they see matter as point sources of energy or as tiny building stones—are not merely subject to an error in logic that can be refuted. True spiritual science has nothing to do with purely theoretical concepts. It is concerned with reality. Anyone looking for more than phenomena in the outside world is on the road not only to logical error but to organic illness affecting the whole of his person. We should not say that to follow this road is an error in logic. We should say that anyone searching for truth in that direction is on the road to organic illness, on the road to feeblemindedness. Spiritual science working towards anthroposophy often has to change theoretical views into views that relate to reality. The search for clarity of ideas and concepts has nothing to do with merely agreeing or disagreeing with the views of others; it has to do with sickness and health, very real things in our lives. It therefore has to be said that a seeker who looks to phenomena for more than mere phenomena, for physical matter, is on the road to feeble-mindedness, to organic illness. This is entirely within the sphere of reality.

In the same way we cannot simply oppose people who look to find abstract spirituality within themselves. Someone looking for the spirit by following the path of mere one-sided inner mysticism, failing to realize that when he comes to see through the tissue of this mysticism it is materiality he finds, is on the way to becoming infantile, to developing an organic illness taking the form of childishness. (I have given it the name that may well be given when one perceives this from beyond the threshold.) If we call this the threshold from the physical to the non-physical world, with the Guardian of the Threshold standing there, the quality we call inspiration, or genius, on this side may justifiably be called childishness on the other side of the threshold. Childishness goes the wrong way in the physical world if it persists throughout life. Genius on the other hand means that a certain childlike quality persists in the background throughout life. Genius is achieved when we are able to retain into ripe old age a quality of soul that normally belongs to childhood. This is seen in its true form from beyond the threshold. If however that childlike soul quality persists one-sidedly into subsequent life stages, then this element, which in its rightful place in the human sphere is genius, becomes childishness instead. Once again we see that purely logical ideas must be replaced with ideas relating to reality as soon as we enter the sphere of spiritual science. They must be replaced with concepts that not merely change our views but produce inner organic changes.

Spiritual science working towards anthroposophy is a very serious matter. The seriousness of it is not given full recognition when people approach the work of spiritual science with their ordinary mental attitudes. They want to agree or disagree the way they usually do in the outside world; they want to continue in their habitual ways as they approach spiritual science. Spiritual science working towards anthroposophy can however only be taught by speaking in the terms of the world beyond. There words have entirely different meanings. Gravity, which exerts a downward pull here on earth, exerts an upward pull in that world. In the spiritual world we have to speak of what draws us down in a way that makes it the exact opposite. It is not surprising then that anyone taking spiritual science seriously is, to begin with, completely misunderstood by people who want to proceed in the customary way—a way that was inevitable in the age of materialism—when they approach spiritual science. The inevitable result is that things like those I dared to put to you yesterday are misunderstood.

Someone presenting his own views in opposition to Oswald Spengler would simply refute him. A spiritual scientist finds himself obliged not to refute Spengler's view in the usual way. He has to assume points of view rather than follow a rigid line; he will have to say that Oswald Spengler speaks from a different point of view, one that offers no prospects for the immediate future. We do justice to such phenomena if we do not simply refute them but show the genius that is in them, speaking with inner concern about the things one would like to see overcome. Spiritual science has much more to do with the way in which we deal with these things than with bald statements, with the kind of mystical platitude that the person who produces it even believes to be a particularly inspired truth. We have to consider these things, for we are moving into an age where we have to get beyond the mere contents of intellectual life. This is something I want to stress over and over again: we must get beyond the mere content of intellectual life.

Going just by the content, even a fool would find it relatively easy to refute Oswald Spengler's ideas. That is by no means difficult, but it is not what matters. What matters is to establish the concrete reality of Spengler's work and show how it can be overcome in a real and concrete way. In future the essential point in characterizing a person will be more and more to consider what they are actually saying rather than to respond in sympathy or antipathy to what he or she has to say. We should not consider whether certain contents please or displease us, but whether there is a spiritual quality to them. It is more important for the overall outcome of world evolution that there is someone who is an inspired materialist, a genius in representing materialism, for that calls for a brilliant mind whilst it often needs very little intelligence to represent platitudinous mysticism. A platitudinous mystic may on occasion do more to make the world materialistic than an inspired materialist. It is the quality of mind that matters. Recognition of this fact will count for much more in future than the actual content. This is something we have to learn. We must not seek for the spirit as though it were a system of logic; we must look for its reality. Let me ask you this. Would it not be possible for you to see that more of the spirit is alive in an inspired materialist than in a spiritualist full of platitudes? These are the things spiritual science working towards anthroposophy must come to see clearly. It is the reality of the spirit that matters, not the abstract statements made by one person or another. People fail to realize how important it is to consider realities and not theories!

Some of the things we see in ordinary life simply must be considered from the point of view of spiritual science today if we are to get them clear in our minds. Consider the parties which have formed in public life in our everyday world. Let us first of all consider the ordinary political parties. You know that the most miserable, sterile cliches are to be found in party politics. Yet to some extent we are all part of this, willy-nilly, unless we want to withdraw completely from public life or perhaps cannot have a vote because we are stateless and have not been given the right to vote anywhere. Everybody who has the right to vote is forced to support one line or another, i.e. to work along party lines. Parties are a fact of life. They go back to better times, to the English see-saw system when there was the Conservative Party on one side and the Liberal Party on the other. It may be said that all the parties that now exist are different combinations of those two shades. Sometimes the liberal element which is to the left takes on some colour from conservatism on the right, and conservatism is coloured with liberalism from the left, as in the case of the Social Democrats, or conservatism turns radical, as we have seen in the present time. All in all it can be said that the conservative-liberal see-saw is the pattern on which all our parties are based. That is the picture one gets when looking at this in an outer way. The most dreadful things are happening in those party organizations—everybody would admit this. The thing exists, however, and the question is why it exists. What does it rally represent? What in fact are parties?

Everything that presents itself in the physical world is an image of the non-physical world. What is it that exists in the non-physical world with the result that in the physical world we have parties as an image of it? The matter can only be properly understood if we grasp the conditions which apply when we go across the threshold to the spiritual world. There we arrive at something very different, at the real nature of things. Here in the physical world we are idealists, sceptics, realists, spiritualists or any other kind of -ists. We are something that can be summed up in a manifesto, as a political or sociological system. In short, we are something-ists. We base ourselves on an abstract notion, for parties always base themselves on manifestos, systems and the like, i.e. on abstract notions. As soon as we cross the threshold to the spiritual world we are no longer dealing in mere logic and abstract notions, we are dealing with realities. It is merely that this is not usually taken seriously. You cannot give your allegiance to a party programme when you have gone past the Guardian of the Threshold, you can only hold to the essential spirit of things, for there everything has to do with the essential spirit. You can merely hold to a spirit of the higher hierarchies and say: That is the one I follow, the one I unite with. Let others present their affairs in their own way, I am uniting with that one, I take his side. The term 'to side with one or another' achieves very real significance then; it is no longer merely abstract. Being human we are inclined to say that as soon as we look beyond the threshold we find three essential spirits: the Christ, Ahriman and Lucifer. It is of course possible to prepare oneself carefully to gain comprehension of the spiritual world and then to say: I choose Christ's party, or Ahriman's or Lucifer's party. It is however also possible to obscure the issue, being badly prepared, and choose Ahriman but call him Christ. We follow a spiritual entity, however—everything is of the essence beyond the threshold! We are always dealing with realities there, not with anything by way of a programme or system.

These words I say to characterize the relationship of the human being to the non-physical world are weighty words. In one particular respect it is not yet possible to say the final word on the subject, because that would be too provocative. Very few people on this earth however are aware that basically it is an illusion to follow party lines, to accept the abstract notions of parties. There is no reality to it and when we begin to follow something that is real we must in fact follow something that lies in the spiritual world beyond the threshold. There is however one party that may immediately be characterized as being well aware of this secret and indeed acting upon it. This was said in public in the course of lectures given at Karlsruhe in 1911[52] and has brought me the hatred of the party in question. These are the Jesuits. They know very well that to follow a party programme— forgive me for using a term commonly used in Germany—is nonsense. One follows a spiritual entity in the non-physical world! That is why their exercises start with the Jesuit having to visualize the spirit whom he is to follow in the Society of Jesus, forming a military corporation for him. When I say that the last word cannot yet be said, I want to hold back concerning the nature of what is called 'Jesus' there. The point is to show that Jesuitism forms a party that follows a spiritual entity and that Jesuits are very well aware that to follow some party or other that goes no further than a programme to be followed in the physical world is a nonsense. The effectiveness of the Society of Jesus is due to the fact that it trains its followers to be the soldiers of a spiritual entity. The do not say this is right and this is wrong. They say: 'It is part of the mission of the spiritual entity I am following;

I shall defend it. I shall oppose anything that is not part of the mission of the spiritual entity I am following, even if it is logically defensible; it is just as possible to defend what Lucifer and Ahriman are about as it is to defend the things Christ is about. There are exactly three logical defences and they are all equally valid.'

We therefore have the strange phenomenon that the Jesuits are of course aware that anthroposophy is taking a spiritual line that is wholly defensible and yet they oppose it. They know full well that logical argument is no effective opposition, for it merely means playing with logic. They know that they are facing an adversary in this battle of minds and they will use all available means. It is therefore pointless to join battle by refuting the refutations of the Jesuits. They know exactly what objections we can raise; the fact that they know them and consider them to be fair makes no difference, however, for they follow another spirit than the one anthroposophy must now follow for the weal of humankind. As soon as one is in the realm of the spirit it is reality that counts. What counts is that one really gets a clear understanding of the spiritual paths, using the whole human being in arriving at such understanding—which certainly can be achieved with healthy common sense nowadays—and not the human dwarf who tends to be the end product of the kind of educational establishments we have today.

The parties which exist in physical life are therefore caricatures of something that rightfully exists in the spiritual world. That is what is so difficult about it. Things appearing in the physical world may be a reflection of something of genuine significance in the spiritual world. In the physical world it is pernicious and abominable, because every world has its own laws, and today we face the growing necessity to work our way up into the spiritual world again. The first stage consists of caricatures of spiritual life appearing in physical life; of people setting up party banners and following party idols when in fact they should be giving their allegiance to spiritual entities. It is truth and reality when it occurs in the non-physical world, and a lie and illusion when it occurs here in the physical world. You see I am not using empty words when I tell you that what matters is to transform purely theoretical things into the reality whenever we wish to speak of the truths that exist beyond the threshold.

Mere refutation of materialism will not achieve anything, because the situation is like this where the human being is concerned: In their whole make-up human beings are really spirit and soul. This element of spirit and soul exists even before we are conceived, before we are born. It has evolved out of our previous earth incarnation; it has gone through the spiritual world. It now assumes flesh, creating a physical image of itself that consists of nervous system, skeletal system, blood system. So we now have two things: the human being in soul and spirit and the human being of flesh and bone that is its image. When we are thinking the usual abstract thoughts, what is it that thinks in us? Not the human being of soul and spirit. It is particularly when we think abstract thoughts, above all using earthly logic, that the physical brain in us is thinking. It is important to know that when materialists say that the brain does the thinking they are quite correct as far as abstract thoughts ar concerned. The physical brain is an image of the spiritual brain, and this image creates an image, abstract thinking being merely an image. It may thus be said that when it comes to abstract ideas the physical brain does the thinking.

This is simply a special case of what I have said before. Materialism has merely found out that the brain is thinking the thoughts that from the middle of the 15th century onwards have become standard in Western civilization. The materialism presented by Moleschott, Buechner and that fat man Vogt[28] cannot be simply refuted by saying it is wrong. It is quite appropriate for human beings who, from the middle of the 15th century onwards, have turned more and more to mere materialism. Human beings of the Western world are in the process of becoming beings that think only with the physical brain. The prophets of such physical brain thinking, Moleschott and Buechner, merely stated what Western humankind was going to be. They were wrong only in so far as they applied this to humankind as a whole. What they said applies only to people living after the middle of the 15th century, and in their case it does apply. People have got used to thinking only with their brains; it is the common way of thinking nowadays. Everything to be found in our ordinary literature, in the whole of modern science, is material thinking, is that kind of thinking. The materialists are quite right, and we could say that Buechner and Vogt would have been unfair to their colleagues if they had said that they thought with the spirit. That is not the case; they think merely with their brains. This cannot be argued against, and it has to be recognized that the road to materiality is not merely a false philosophy but something with a very real effect. That is also the reason why, when something like spiritual science working towards anthroposophy appears on the scene, those people will say: 'These are thoughts beyond comprehension; they cannot be grasped.' Well, they want to think with their brains: the thoughts of spiritual science are however thought with a soul and spirit element that has torn itself away from the brain. People must make efforts to tear their soul and spirit away from the brain with the help of thoughts that have been produced in this way; they must think those thoughts through. People must make an effort to think those thoughts through, to use the opportunity that still exists of tearing the element of soul and spirit away from the physical aspect of the brain. This element is on the way to being chained to the physical brain. People must tear themselves free. It is not a question therefore of right views and wrong views but of a process. The thoughts of spiritual science working towards anthroposophy are given to the world in the hope that people who are still capable of handling the old faculty of tearing themselves away that lies in them, will indeed make use of it and try and understand thoughts that are independent of the physical body, so that their souls may grow free of the body. It is therefore a question of having the will to understand anthroposophy; anthroposophy is intended to tear the element of spirit and soul away from the physical body. Our mission therefore is not merely to refute views that are wrong; but we must face the fact that very many people want to slither into them, want to be sheer matter and want to think, use their will and feel out of matter. We want to give spiritual science working towards anthroposophy to the world as something real, so that spirit and soul may be torn away from matter. The aim is to prevent the possibility of people losing their spirit and soul, for they now run the risk of slithering entirely into the ahrimanic sphere. People face the risk of losing soul and spirit and of losing themselves as human beings when the material world vanishes into nothingness, as I have described on an earlier occasion.

It is not a question therefore of replacing the old with the new, but to become active in the search for truth. This saves the soul from slithering into mere materiality; it saves the spirit and soul element from slithering into the ahrimanic sphere, where egoity would be lost. It is not a question therefore of refuting materialism, but of saving humankind from materialism coming true. Materialism is in the process of developing into something that is true rather than false. When people say that materialism is wrong they are not talking about what really matters. No, we have to say that materialism is coming to be more and more right; in our present culture it is coming to be more and more right. We may well find that by the beginning of the 3rd millenium humankind will have developed in such a way that materialism is the correct view. It is not a question of refuting materialism, for it is in the process of becoming right. It is a question of making it not right, because it is on the way to becoming a fact and no longer merely a wrong theory.

Certain people are trying to ignore these things. They want to make it as easy as possible for others, telling them to see how wrong materialism is and inviting them to turn to an abstract mysticism that will give them everything they need. We could take up such abstract mysticism, but that would encourage materialism to become real and not mere theory. We do not have to overcome materialism because it is wrong, using words that remain theory; we have to overcome it because it is right and we must fight against it being the right thing. This puts another face on things, and this is also where we find ourselves in the reality of the spiritual world—not with theories, but with a living approach to the truth that in the cosmic scheme of things is an active deed. People find it unpalatable to have to listen to such things, yet that is the light in which everything should be regarded, even individual events. Believe me, the old methods of combat are finished with; everything that could be the habitual way in the past is now finished. We must consider things in the light of the spirit.

What is conservatism? What is liberalism? Here on earth they are caricatures of the spiritual world. Conservatives are followers of Ahriman, liberals of Lucifer. Having passed the Guardian of the Threshold one can see how the whole of conservatism is running after Ahriman and the whole of liberalism after Lucifer. That may seem peculiar to the sophisticated people of today. It is however because this seems so peculiar that spiritual science working towards anthroposophy is so difficult to understand. We shall never understand spiritual science by merely thinking it; we shall only come to understand it if every one of its concepts makes us suffer and rejoice, when we feel lifted up and cast down, when we want to despair over a word, or think we shall be redeemed because of a word, when we see destiny at work in what normally appears as a shadowy theory just as we see it at work in things that are done in the outside world, when what spiritual science working towards anthroposophy has to say goes beyond being mere words and becomes reality. Then, when the inner impulse alive in this spiritual science is understood and felt, it will be rightly seen why things that for a time were maintained as mere theory, because people first had to come to know about them, must now become reality, why we have to be serious about the reality that lives in the words of spiritual science working towards anthroposophy. It will be seen that the necessity arises in our age to make the substantial essence of those words come to reality.

It is still the case that what is really intended with such a Waldorf School is not at all seen in the light of reality, that it is far too little considered in the sense which I have tried to characterize for you. Believe me, this is not to touch your hearts, nor to gain a little more support. Things have been said that had to be said now because humankind must know them. That is why I have said the things I have been saying. I merely wish that the opportunity would arise to say these things to a sufficiently large number of people, so that these people develop an inner impulsiveness where they take words as realities and do not merely listen in the belief that one is speaking theories.

This is what I have wanted to put to you on these two occasions. It will have to happen that outer events follow not on the external contents of spiritual science as it is presented, but out of inner impulses. Fighters like the Jesuits know very well what many followers of anthroposophy still fail to realize: that spiritual science working towards anthroposophy is a reality. Since they have come to realize this—they have done so for some time now, from about 1906 or 1907—since they have come to realize it they are opposing this spiritual science with increasing vigour. Many anthroposophists have no idea of the methods that are used, the sheer ingenuity, because there is a refusal to be really sure in one's mind of the seriousness of the situation. Words will only evoke a little bit of the things one really wishes people to take to heart; I have tried, however, to present just a little of it to you on these two occasions. If we reflect on what has been said, if we progress from reflection to feeling, to letting it become part of the whole of our being, there will be an end to abstract mysticism and to modern science. It will become the essential inner nature of the human being, it will be the power that releases spirit and soul again from physical matter, it will overcome a materialism that unfortunately is not wrong but is indeed true.

Stuttgart, 21 September 1920

As you are well aware, it is often said today that spiritual science cannot have anything to do with real knowledge, with genuine perception, and that it can only be a matter of faith, a subjective way of believing things to be true. This kind of attitude then leads to a distinction being made between knowledge and belief, as is the general custom. A frequent objection raised against spiritual science working towards anthroposophy is that a kind of subjective knowledge that really can only be a matter of belief—perhaps one should not even call it knowledge but merely the subjective belief that something is true—is to be elevated, jumped up, to the level of certain and exact knowledge, to the level of a genuine science.

This distinction that is made between science and belief is quite a recent development. The view is that science should only concern itself with things perceptible to the senses, or at most with things that can be established and explored on the basis of experiments, and that certain knowledge can solely and exclusively come from such depths. Belief is seen as going beyond the physical realm and it is said that one should never assume that anything that is the subject of belief can be transformed into certain knowledge. Thus we have science on one side, a science limited to the physical world, and a supersensible, non-physical world on the other that may be accepted by anyone who finds it acceptable but cannot be known with certainty and must remain a matter of subjective faith.

Anyone who takes life seriously really ought to feel that the supposed distinction made by so many people between knowledge and belief poses a riddle which must be solved. Fundamentally speaking, however, only initiation science can genuinely show the reason for the efforts that are being made at the present time— and indeed have already been made for a long time, for centuries—to teach humankind the difference between knowledge of the finite, transitory realm of the senses and belief in something that is infinite, permanent, supersensible. You know that everything that is presented here from the point of view of spiritual science working towards anthroposophy is thoroughly scientific in spirit and asks to be considered as fully equal to the science relating to the physical world. It represents knowledge, perception, of the supersensible. Initiation knowledge has to look far back into human evolution, however, if it is to help us understand why in the present age humankind has been taught that there is such a difference between knowledge and faith.

Going back a long way in human evolution we come to a time when people had a primal knowledge—we have discussed this a number of times—that was inherited from the gods, as it were. Such things as proof, as demonstrating the truth of something, were not known then. Knowledge came to people at that time when a power arose in their hearts and minds that was not the power of empty, abstract thinking, or something like that, but a power filled with divine light substance, divine life substance, that felt itself to be in communion with divine worlds. Human beings knew that they were connected with divine spheres; they felt this and perceived it the way we perceive colours and sounds outside us. There was no need for proof, for there was perception of the immediate presence. People knew nothing of proof, nor of logical demonstration. All they knew was that as human beings they were filled with what the gods instilled into them. This certainly was 'knowledge' in the earliest stages of human evolution, and it had to do with perception of the divine origin of human beings. Knowing themselves to be united with the gods, and being given the power by their initiates to look up to this union with the gods, people were also aware of the divine origin of man. They were aware that humankind had descended to earth from the world where it had existed as soul and spirit. The divine and spiritual origin of humankind was taken as a matter of course when this primal knowledge existed all over the globe in the early times of human evolution.

This primal knowledge had to develop further, however. If it had remained as it was, people would in a sense have continued to be filled with the divine spirit for ever, but they could not have achieved freedom, the ability to make free decisions. As soon as their arms moved, they would have had to say: 'A god within me is moving my arms.' When they were walking, they would have had to say: 'A god within me is moving my feet.' Those early human beings certainly felt like that. They felt, as it were, that a divine spirit was present inside their skin. That is also the origin of the idea that the human body is a temple. In early times a human being was indeed like the earthly home of a god who who descended to earth to take up his abode among human beings. Human beings had to become independent, however. As a result this primal divine knowledge gradually faded and the divine heritage grew less and less. To achieve freedom, human beings had to develop knowledge, perception, thinking, feeling and will activity out of their own resources. In a way the gods abandoned them, but it was for their own good, if I may put it like this. Divine knowledge withdrew so that human knowledge might develop. In later times the whole path to be taken by the divine knowledge that had once existed all over the globe, the path to earthly and human knowledge, had to be watched over from the mystery centres. It was the task of initiates to regulate the way humankind were to be trained, as it were, so that human beings would find the right way of growing out of that ancient divine knowledge and into earthly and human knowledge.

At a time when much of the original divine knowledge had faded and the mysteries had assumed the task of guiding human beings—by and large instructing them in such a way that the right transition could be made from primal wisdom to human knowledge and ultimately freedom—it happened that a certain number of people came together from the far reaches of the earth to look for a way in which the purpose of guiding humankind in the right way, purposes originating in the mystery centres, could be crossed. Human associations were formed, in a way, that considered it their mission to go against the proper course of progress. We really have to use spiritual science if we want to consider the activity of a widespread association of human beings in post-primeval times. History does not go that far back and there are no documents to bear outer witness to that time. Such an association developed and adopted the mystery knowledge in a certain way, still using the methods that had been employed in the mysteries to maintain contact with the divine source and origin. By that time however the mystery centres where honest work was being done had long since been concentrating on guiding the transition from the divine knowledge of the ancients to human and earthly knowledge. Thus there was a time in earthly history when the rightful representatives of mystery knowledge were totally involved in guiding the transition from the divine knowledge of the ancients to human and earthly knowledge. That was the healthy feeling and attitude, healthy for that time. Mingled into this was an element arising because a well organized association wanted to restore to humankind an antiquated primal divine knowledge at a time when it was out of date, when the murmur of ancient divine knowledge was no longer supposed to reach human ears. At a time when they had grown beyond the state where they had divine knowledge, people found that there was a group that still wanted the old knowledge to be widely accessible.

Why did the members of this association in post-primeval times want such a thing? They wanted to strike at the root, as it were, of the knowledge then evolving. They did not want humanity to achieve freedom. Efforts were indeed made in post-primeval times to prevent humankind from developing the faculties that would lead to freedom, and for that purpose the aim was to strike at the root of earthly and physical knowledge. These people, who may be called the 'enemies' of human evolution in post-primeval times, made the distinction between human knowledge and divine knowledge, a divine knowledge that was no longer legitimate at the time. To deluge human beings with divine knowledge, which they had grown out of by that time, meant to induce a dreamy, visionary state of conscious awareness. Vast masses of people lived in that kind of fanciful, visionary state in post-primeval times. Their inclinations to develop human knowledge were stifled. The reason why human knowledge came to be so deficient in many respects as time went on—I have given many examples of this—and why defects have even crept into the development of speech and language, was that a form of divine knowledge was presented to people in a way that appealed to their vanity.

Let us investigate the influences that made people endeavour to befog the minds of the masses and strike at the root of the new knowledge that was evolving and also at the root of a language that arose from the depths of human nature. It has to be said that the individuals concerned were totally under the influence of luciferic powers. Luciferic powers were alive in them, luciferic powers that did not want human thinking, feeling and will activity to descend as far as the earth, as it were. Human beings were supposed to grow more and more physical, but these individuals wanted to keep them spiritual, to stop them from achieving their mission on earth. The individuals concerned were the spiritualists of post-primeval times. They were against human progress. The divine intention was that human beings should find ways of letting their souls and spirits enter more and more deeply into physical bodies. The individuals of whom I am speaking wanted to prevent this, however. Considering this in present-day terms—because it is difficult to give an accurate characterization of the state human beings had reached during the post-primeval period—we might say that more than a little of a certain unconscious untruthfulness was apparent in those individuals. The impulse to descend into the material world, to make it part of oneself, had of course been given through the mysteries. The Lucifer-dominated individuals of post-primeval times certainly could not deny this. They therefore did not call themselves 'spiritualists' but actually 'protagonists of the material world'—to put it in present-day terms; these words would have to be translated into the terms in which people thought in primeval times. They told people: 'You will come to materiality if you follow us, if you make use of the power we provide in the form of later divine knowledge, if you use it to strengthen your soul and spirit. You will then find yourselves the conquerers of all that this earth holds for you; you will conquer the earth quickly and easily when you have a share in the power of the gods.' The Lucifer-dominated leaders of certain parts of humanity gave themselves the honourable title 'fighters for the material world.'

Those individuals created a certain schism between human evolution as it was intended and the wrong notions which they presented to humanity, notions that the ideal was to conquer materiality rather than coming to be at home in it gradually. They said people should make certain divine powers their own by having supersensible knowledge at the wrong time, and that they should use this knowledge to conquer the material world that is perceptible to the senses.

Today we have the reverse picture of what existed in those primeval times. Certain confessions have started to oppose the regular progress of science, the acquisition of knowledge. Science has had its roots damaged, as it were. The result is that science and language show certain defects throughout the course of Earth evolution. Science has nevertheless come about, for sufficient numbers of people who were under the influence of the true mysteries and corrupted initiation knowledge stood up against the individuals whose real aim was to strike at the root of knowledge and eradicate it. Science has come about. It has taken the road I have often characterized in detail. It reached the level it did by the middle of the 15th century, when the fifth post-Atlantean epoch began, and it has continued to the present time. According to present-day initiation knowledge, however, science has now reached a further turning point. Today it is ripe to enter into human freedom, as it were. Essentially modern science still considers only physical things to be valid and exact; it is only prepared to consider things that are perceptible to the senses or may be established on the basis of experiments. As I have often said, this science is now ripe to develop to a point where it can grasp Imagination, the inspired, the intuitive world; where it can find its ways to experience, to grasp the spirit. This science is ordained to grow and in growing to assume the form of spiritual vision. It is ripe for this today.

For the regular progress of science it will however be necessary for humanity to develop an inner attitude that wants to use the same conscientious approach to investigation and research that is used in botany, physics, chemistry and so on to explore the outer world of the senses and make outer science triumph. People must want to use that same attitude when it comes to the inner life of human beings. We must want the attitude and approach used in outer science to be transformed into a way of taking hold of the supersensible world in a living way. I have pointed the way in my *Knowledge of the Higher Worlds*, in *Occult Science*[53] and other books of this kind. It has to be clearly understood that the true aim we have at the bottom of our hearts, the only viable aim for spiritual science working towards anthroposophy, differs from Jesuitism, which is more or less its polar opposite. The difference is that Jesuitism in particular wants to keep science, knowledge as such, at the level of pure experimentation and observation. Take a look—but a careful look—at the scientific literature from Jesuit sources. The approach, the way of thinking, is as materialistic as it can be. It aims to keep knowledge entirely in the world of the senses, and strictly separate the knowledge that can only be obtained by observation based on the physical senses and by experimentation from anything that is a matter of belief or revelation. The reasoning is that no bridge shall ever be built between outer knowledge or science and anything to do with faith. Spiritual science working towards anthroposophy on the other hand is aiming to do just that, to find the way from a science of the physical, sense-perceptible world to a science of the spirit. This science of the spirit would however apply the same stringent standards as the outer science of the sense-perceptible world.

The picture, then, is as follows: The science of the physical, sense-perceptible world is the root. Supersensible knowledge is to evolve from the same impulses that govern botany, physics, chemistry and so on, except that they will be applied in a different field. In certain quarters it was foreseen that this was to come. It was however in the interests of these people to prevent it happening, and they therefore introduced something into human evolution that now presents itself as a sharp contrast. This is the sharp contrast I have spoken of earlier: the distinction made between ancient ways of knowing that in the regular course of events became human knowledge, human science, and a divine knowledge used to drug human minds. The sharp distinction between knowledge and belief was presented to human minds and the true aim turned into its opposite. Knowledge of the sense-perceptible world was to be firmly retained and given great emphasis. It simply has to be admitted that Jesuit literature on materialistic science is extraordinarily brilliant in the clarity of its reasoning, its sheer readability. The Jesuit literature on the material world is much more brilliantly written than the works of many others writers on the subject today. Father Erich Wasmann's[54] work on ants, for example, is really good, you will gain more from reading it than from the pedantic, uninspired writings of other scientists. Many more examples could be given. The [work of the] Jesuits would be excellent if they confined themselves to the material world; it is a deliberate aim [of the Jesuits] to use their description of the material world to encourage people to associate knowledge with the materialistic aspect of the physical world only. The intention is to pretend to human minds that the methods used to gain knowledge cannot be used to investigate the supersensible world. In ancient times Lucifer-dominated individuals suggested that human beings would gain mastery of the world if they made use of ancient divine knowledge, yet evolution had already gone beyond this point. Now we have late followers of those people from post-primeval times pretending to the world that it is not possible to extend knowledge to the supersensible sphere and that knowledge cannot go beyond the sense-perceptible world. In those early times the intention had been to drug people with supersensible knowledge. Now human beings of the same ilk want to use all possible means to push humanity into the physical world; they want human beings to be stuck in that world and grasp the supersensible world only with the nebulous impulse of faith. In post-primeval times the aim had been to inundate humankind with an excess of supersensible knowledge. Today those late followers want human beings to have less than the right amount of knowledge in this sphere. Past intent was to provide supersensible knowledge that was no longer appropriate. Present intent is to let people have only sense-bound knowledge, making the supersensible world an area where every individual may hold whatever views he or she likes.

What would be the outcome if the group of people to whom we are referring were to achieve some kind of victory? These are the people who deliberately make a sharp distinction between knowledge and belief. There are of course large numbers of easily led people who come across the diatribe on the 'clear distinction between faith and knowledge' and repeat it; they merely repeat it. What is all this about? The aim is to do the opposite of what those individuals in post-primeval times did in their way. In the old days the intention was to prevent humanity from descending completely and taking up its mission on earth. Today the intention is to keep people tied to that mission on earth to prevent their further development, for which the earth would provide the basis. The very people who are now supporting materialism call themselves 'spiritualists', or priests of some faith or other, representatives of the supersensible world. In those ancient times the people offering a life in the spirit that was no longer justifiable called themselves materialists. They did so from the point of view which I have characterized. Today a large number of people who really wish to keep humanity bound to the material world call themselves representatives of the spiritual world. The most powerful source of materialism today does not lie in the ideas put forward by Buechner, Moleschott or Vogt. The most powerful source is Rome and anything that is in any way connected with this centre of materialism. They achieved their aims not by saying: 'I want to encourage materialism', but by keeping people bound to materialism. This is done by letting them develop faith merely as a nebulous impulse towards supersensible spheres and making sure that no impulse enters into humanity that could lead to comprehension of the supersensible sphere. The idea that Rome might lead the way in conquering the supersensible sphere for humanity is *the* historical untruth of the present age. This must be clearly and firmly understood. It must also be understood that Protestantism as it has evolved out of Roman Catholicism in recent times contains much that is of Roman Catholic origin. The desire to keep supersensible knowledge nebulous by making it a matter of faith, so that people cannot comprehend the supersensible world, has strongly persisted in the Protestant church. Quite apart from this, the signs of the times may be read to indicate clearly that Rome will overcome the Protestant element, and Rome will continue to make great efforts in the direction I have characterized.

So you see that if one wishes to achieve something in the world that goes against the normal progress of humanity one calls oneself by the opposite name, as it were. Humanity must learn to get beyond putting its trust in mere names, and it is indeed in the process of doing so. Humanity must go to deeper sources than merely living in words and phrases. Basically this is already beginning to happen. Imagine someone calls and you are brought a visiting card on which it says 'Ernest Miller'. Surely you would not expect to see somone come through the door whose clothes are covered in flour. Nor would you expect 'Richard Smith' to come straight from shoeing horses. If you have lived in a village you may still recall people saying 'There comes the miller'—and that would have been a genuine miller—or 'There comes the smith', meaning a real blacksmith. There names were still more than an outer label. The names we bear have taken a road where it is no longer possible to draw conclusions as to the nature of the individual who calls himself by a particular name. The words that make up people's names give no clue as to the essential characteristics of the person or persons concerned. The name Smith does not tell us whether the person called by that name is a smith or not, nor can we conclude someone is a miller when we hear that his name is Miller. That is the road names have taken. The rest of the language will follow the same road, and people will have to learn to develop their ideas on principles other than words or phrases. You can draw no conclusions as to the nature of a person from the fact that his visiting card says he is Mr Miller. In the same way you will have to get used to the fact that the characteristics of words will not tell you what your ideas about the world ought to be.

If you seriously act in a way that is in accord with the urgent necessity of the present time you find yourself little understood. If I were to present the things I have to present by way of spiritual science in a way that meets the modern desire for scientific terminology, I would not be doing what I have in fact always made efforts to do. This is to present a subject from all kinds of different angles, sometimes more in their material aspect and at other times more in their spiritual aspect, always remembering the principle which Goethe expressed as follows: 'The truth will certainly never be found exactly half-way between two contradictory statements.'[55] At the stage we have now reached in our evolution it simply is no longer possible to think that a particular content can be adequately defined by using words to give a one-sided characterization. The subject has to be characterized from different aspects, and the procedure used to characterize it in words must be similar to that used to make a photographic record of a tree, for instance, by taking pictures of it from a variety of angles. The photographs will look very different, but putting them together one sees something that conveys the tree as a whole.

Read the various courses of lectures and you will see that I have adhered to the principle and presented the subject matter from many different angles. If we wish to present the things human beings need today, things that will serve the progress of humankind, we must get into the habit of proceeding in this way. There are certain groups of people who are against this and want to continue to use rigid terminology. Human concerns cannot be defined in rigid terms and that is why we now see forms of socialism developing that want to go further into terminology definition but can only lead to destruction. Concerning events in Eastern Europe, people think the danger has passed now that the Poles have won; before that the Bolsheviks had the upper hand for a time, but the whole has been the most dreadful tragicomedy of human behaviour. The present war between Russia and Poland provides a good demonstration of the extent to which human beings have lost their moral fibre today.

My book *Towards Social Renewal*[31] was genuinely based on the social life of the present time and the style was chosen to meet the needs of this present-day life. Yet people come and ask for word definitions more or less the way words are defined in most schoolbooks nowadays—much to the detriment of education and training. Words have more and more come away from the original inner experience, and it is increasingly necessary to draw one's conclusions as to the reality from other sources than the words used. After all, when we hear the name Miller we do not base our conclusions as to the nature of the individual on an analysis of the name Miller but on quite different aspects. It will be necessary for human beings to come away from words and judge the existing world by other criteria.

This had been in preparation for a long time, but it has not always been applied in a sense that would be in accord with human evolution. The outcome has been that widespread societies now say: 'We declare ourselves for Christ', yet after all the word used need not apply to the spirit they say they are worshipping. The point is not that something or other is called the Christ and that people have ideas about this Christ. The point is the real nature of the spirit towards whom human feelings are turning. And if one develops a very mundane image of this Christ, if one even undergoes militaristic initiation during one's training to learn how the soul has to be prepared before one forms an idea of the Christ, if one is shown the image of Jesus the King, seeing oneself and other followers as King Jesus' army, it may happen that having created such a material image of Christ one then gives the name of Christ to quite a different spirit. The truth is that one's soul is then turned towards quite a different spirit who is wrongfully called Christ. This happens a great deal nowadays and it happens in such a way that people sometimes have a peculiar awareness of it.

Many years ago I had a conversation in Marburg one day with a Protestant clergyman who had travelled a great deal.[56] We talked of the way the real idea of the Christ has gradually disappeared from modern theology, of the way this modern theology is on the one hand using certain initiation ceremonies to bring Christ down and make Him a physical Jesus even in the picture one has of Him, and how on the other hand certain theologians see Christ only as the 'simple man of Nazareth'. This Protestant theologian, a man who had travelled widely and seen something of the world, then said to me: 'The younger generation of theologians really no longer have the Christ, they really should no longer called themselves Christians or followers of Christ; they really ought to call themselves Jesuits, except that that name already has another meaning, because all they are left with is Jesus.' Those were not my views but the views of a Protestant theologian who has travelled a great deal. To stop you from developing prejudices and taking too poor a view of theologians, let me add that the man was a Swabian and was also married to a Swabian, a lady from Stuttgart to boot. That is just to stop you from getting prejudiced.

We have tried to see how the separation of knowledge and belief came about. This separation of knowledge and belief also prevents people from knowing that there is a life before birth, or before conception. I also spoke of this yesterday.[57] All that is permitted is belief in life *post mortem*, i.e. after death, for that is an idea that can be presented to human minds even if one reckons only with egotistical elements in the human soul. The concept of life before birth, the life we have gone through between our last death and our birth into the present life, needs perceptive insight if it is to be grasped; it is no good putting one's money on egotistical soul instincts if one wishes to teach it. The way people are here on earth is that they do not care to know what they have gone through before; egotistical reasons make them interested to know what will happen after death, however. It is easy to preach on what people may expect after death, therefore, for that appeals to the egotistical instincts in their souls. It is difficult to preach on life before birth; instead one must assume that human beings desire to know the truth and want to live a life that is worthy of human beings. This will of course lead us to see education and then also the whole of life on earth in a new light. Life on earth must be seen as the fulfilling of a mission we have been given before we descended from the spiritual world into physical existence.

This new approach that simply must come to be widely accepted in the outside world, an approach that will also have to create new social forms, has many enemies. You can guess this from various hidden trends. I want to end today be telling you something—this is something I am forced to do—of the murky sources and origins of the elements that want to destroy our spiritual science. The sheer effrontery is staggering and there will be more and more of this unless souls come awake to a much greater degree than has been the case until now.

You know, and our friends here have fought against it, that the abominable slander has been spread about all over Germany and beyond of German officers being betrayed to the Entente due to the efforts of the Threefold Order people and so forth.[58] I have recently been supplied with copies of some of the abominable documents that are widely distributed at present—fake letters reputedly written by our people, cunningly designed to spread the most dreadful slander, and faked interviews. Their character will be obvious to you as soon as I tell you that one of them concludes with the words: 'D.H. is not in fact part of the Steiner fraternity. He has merely infiltrated the organization to spy on them, to get on to their tricks. He has reported his findings to a small group of patriotic people, and the word is that Steiner is committing high treason and is in league with the Entente.' That is just a small sample of the murky work that is being done, and it it much more widespread than you would think.

Another very pretty example comes from someone in this area[59] whom I once called a swine in a public lecture—because everything this person is instigating against me simply cannot be called by any other name. This person is now using the black art of printing to spread things against me in an article headed 'Threefold Order Plagiarized'. This says no less than that a lady had created a threefold order some time ago. (The lady was not quite careful enough, however, for she failed to find out from the literature that my threefold order was known before that in certain circles; she gives a time that is somewhat later than the time when I was talking to a great many people about the threefold order in question.) This lady, then, is said to have created a threefold order and to have sent the manuscript to a philanthropic society; it is then said to have gone to Hamburg where the person concerned kept it for four weeks rather than two, and that I probably read it in that time and took the threefold idea from that manuscript. Of course the lady cannot very well say that there is any agreement between the threefold order I am presenting and whatever she had put in her manuscript. She therefore maintains that the threefold idea was plagiarized from her manuscript, but that it has been messed about. Oh yes. He's pinched my watch, but that one looks quite different! She has now written a work about her threefold order. According to her this consists of the golden section 'state, cultural sphere, church', with everything again determined by the golden section. So we get a centralized state and within it two parts—exactly the same as postulated in the threefold order; so the threefold order is a botch job.—If you want to get an idea, let me recommend this work to you; the title is *3:5, 5:8 = 21:34. The secret of clearing the debts in reasonable time'* [English rendering of the original German title] by Elisabeth Mathilde Metzdorff-Teschner,[60] published by the author in 1920. Maybe you could make amends by saying: 'We have been working for the threefold order, but we really only did this in Mrs Elizabeth Metzdorff-Teschner's name.' That is another thing she expects of us, and she is writing letters to all kinds of people.

That is Mr Rohm's [59] source, and the things he writes are now reaching Switzerland where they are presented to the people by every Roman Catholic parish priest. No one of course has even the least idea of the actual source. These articles say something very different, and people find it quite easy to believe, for the idiocy at the source of it is not apparent. That is the way people work nowadays and they know very well what they are doing. They are deliberately working against the sincere efforts that are being made to serve the true progress of humankind. In Switzerland it is above all the Roman Catholic parish priests who are using that style, reprinting everything that comes from the centres run by Mr Knapp[61] and others, everything disgorged from the rubbish bins of Mr Rohm and so forth. I cannot help remembering that until recently there have been—and indeed still are—many people even among anthroposophists who are faithful subscribers to Mr Rohm's *Leuchtturm* [Lighthouse]. They keep dishing up Mr Rohm's views, keep coming up with one thing or another.

I am sorry, I had to give you some small samples—there are plenty more—so that you can see the methods that are used.

The strength inherent in spiritual science working towards anthroposophy should give anthroposophy the strength to gain more than just names from words—a feeling for the truth. Once you have a feeling for the truth you will find the road, and it lies in a very different region from what people generally find comfortable in the present time. It is a road to be sought in the kind of way I have described today. It would be more comfortable in this day and age to talk of other things rather than refer to the powerful adversaries who are responsible for distinction being made between knowledge and belief and who aim to block the road by which knowledge of the sense-perceptible world can become knowledge of spheres beyond the senses.

Stuttgart, 8 November 1920

Today we shall base ourselves on facts relating to the nature of human beings and then make the transition to certain guiding principles in world history.

We have already considered the rhythmical alternation betwen sleeping and waking that human beings experience within a twenty-four hour period and have done so from many different points of view. Today I want to take a point of view that has so far been used less frequently in considering this alternation between sleeping and waking.

We know that there are three main aspects to a human being. One aspect is the head organization. Here, we have first of all the sensory organism which faces the outside world. The actual brain organism lies more on the inside. We know of course that this is only an approximate way of looking at these things. We cannot simply divide the human being into sections according to the space occupied. We have to be clear in our minds that the nerves and senses merely have their main concentration in the head and that they are in fact present everywhere in the human being. Everything said in this respect applies to the whole human being. We base our characterization on the part where the main concentration lies, i.e. the head. So we have the sensory organism facing the outside and the brain organism situated inside.

The question is, what happens to the sensory organism and the brain organism when a human being changes from the waking state—which you are familiar with, perhaps not in depth but at least in outer terms—to the sleeping state? As you know, the sensory organism ceases to be active. The brain organism can be observed in so far as our dream life shines into our souls, in a way. If you consider this dream life you will be able to say that it presents you with a kind of surrounding scenery that in some respects is similar to the outside world you perceive with the senses. It contains images from the outside world you perceive with the senses. Human beings know very well when they are awake, that dream life presents them with images that, in a way, derive from the outside world we perceive with the senses. When we then take a closer look at the dream world, considering it in an unbiased way, we find that the dream images are connected—that they relate to each other; they interrelate in a way that is as definite as the interrelations and connections that exist in our waking thoughts, though these tend to be more imageless. It may be said, however, that whereas human beings have full control of the way thoughts are connected in the imageless thinking of their waking life, and are able to use their will to connect one thought with another, this does not apply in the interplay of dream images. Dream images have their own order. Human beings are passive where they are concerned. If we then reflect on the way in which dream images follow each other we find that it is as if the phenomena of ordinary thinking proceed in a watered-down way, as if they lack drive and will. Residues of sensory and also of thought life can still be traced in dream life. It will be evident from everything we discover as we consider our dream life—and spiritual science will be able to establish this beyond all doubt—that the human brain, which in a way is the physical basis of our life of ideas, must have undergone a change from the way it was in the waking state. In the waking state the situation is that our will gives us control of the way thoughts follow each other. In our dream life we have no such control. What is more, our senses have ceased to act and our dream life only contains images that echo the life of the senses. The life of the senses has therefore also been watered down.

The question we want to ask ourselves today is what kind of changes the human brain had undergone. If you take an unbiased view you will have to agree that spiritual science is right when it says that the brain acts like a sense organ when we dream. A sense organ receives impressions of the outside world and immediately processes them, at least to some extent. The way a sense organ faces the outside world does not involve an element of will, however. If you consider the way the sense organs face the outside world and compare this with the dream state you will find that when the brain acts as the physical basis of dreaming—take it as a working hypothesis, if you like, that it provides the physical basis for dreaming—it has come to resemble a sense organ. It has become more of a sense organ than it is in the waking state; or we may also say that it is not a sense organ when we are awake for it shows none of the properties of a sense organ in that state.

Now we do not have far to go to understand what happens in dreamless sleep. Dreams hold a middle position between waking and sleeping. If the brain becomes more like a sense organ even when we are dreaming, it must do so to an even greater extent when we are fully asleep. The way we are constituted as human beings today we are not in a position to make use of this sense organ in normal life. There was, however, a time in the history of humankind when human beings were able to use the brain as a sense organ to a very considerable degree. In a way, however, the brain always becomes a sense organ between going to sleep and waking up. We know that, between going to sleep and waking up again, the real human being—the human soul and spirit—is in the outside world. We will not take time at this point to consider the nature of this outside world; we merely need to understand clearly that the essential soul and spirit of the human being is then in an outside world of soul and spirit. The physical world we see around us between waking up and going to sleep does not reveal its spiritual and soul ingredients. In the state which pertains between going to sleep and waking up, the human being is in the outside world which has its soul and spirit aspect. Today the constitution of human beings is such that they experience themselves unconsciously in the outside world of soul and spirit.

This soul and spirit environment in which we find ourselves during sleep was the actual world in those far distant times where the original wisdom of humankind had its origin. An echo of those times is still to be found in the Vedic writings, in Vedanta philosophy—in short in the wisdom that was revealed in the ancient Orient. Looking back to those times we find exactly what those early people of the ancient Orient experienced in the outside world between going to sleep and waking up. For them, the brain was still very much a sense organ when they were asleep. It was a sense organ, however, which did not permit them to think at the same time as they made sensory perceptions. When the people of the ancient Orient were in the world of soul and spirit they were actually able to perceive what they experienced between going to sleep and waking up. In a way this was reflected in their brains, which had become sense organs. They were however unable to think whilst they were in that condition. They had to wait until they were awake, as it were, before they were able to think the things that they had perceived. We actually have outer evidence that things were the way I have just described. You only need to try and enter into anything that still remains of ancient oriental culture and you will find that the wisdom of that culture took the form of representing the universe perceptible to the senses from a spiritual point of view. Astrology, now a mere caricature, was living wisdom in those times. Most of that ancient wisdom was based on the revelations of the stars, the revelations of the night sky, i.e. on things hidden from view between waking up and going to sleep. Human beings experienced these things between going to sleep and waking up. They found themselves in the outer world and their souls and spirits experienced their relationship with the heavenly bodies. When they woke up, their brains changed from being sense organs to a state partly similar to that of our own brains—except that their brains were constituted in such a way that when they were awake they were able to remember what they had experienced during sleep. The things they remembered lit up in their minds as instinctive Imaginations. As people went through their daily lives in the ancient Orient they were able to deflect their inner attention from the sense-perceptible world around them and focus it on the great illuminating pictures their souls perceived as a memory of their night-time experiences. Those were the original oriental Imaginations. Echoes of them are to be found in the Veda and in Vedanta philosophy and literature.

What image did the people of those times have of themselves? It certainly was not the kind of description of the human being that is given in anatomy or physiology today, which is based on the evidence of the senses concerning outer form. At that time human beings experienced themselves as soul and spirit among all the other things they experienced in the outside world between going to sleep and waking up. They experienced a cosmos that was soul and spirit, and themselves as soul and spirit within that cosmos. Exactly how did they experience themselves? They perceived themselves as their own ideal model. Please pay particular attention to these words. When an individual living in those times had an illuminating Imagination of what he had experienced in his sleep, he saw himself as the ideal model of himself and was able to say to himself: 'My ideal model looks like this. This model contains specific models, as it were, of the inside of my head, of my lungs, liver and so on.' People did not have the experience of themselves that we are given on the basis of modern anatomy and physiology, i.e. in terms of organs perceptible to the outer senses. They had experience of the ideal model, the idea out of which the organs perceptible to the senses are created. Human beings had the experience of being heavenly and divine spirits—the heavenly and divine ideal of an earthly human being. They were therefore less interested in the earthly human being than they were in the heavenly and divine ideal.

This whole complex of experiences also led to something else. It helped people to realize that they had, in fact, been those heavenly and divine ideals before they were conceived or born as physical human beings. In ancient oriental times human beings were so constituted that they had the experience of being divine and heavenly human beings, and at the same time experienced themselves as they had been before they became earthly. That is the essential point of ancient oriental cultures. Human beings experienced what they had been before they entered into physical existence on earth. Their conviction of this was only instinctive, but it did give them the firm conviction that they had existed before they came to earth and had descended from a spiritual world into the world of the physical senses. It is a forgotten characteristic of the ancient oriental religions that they were very much concerned with life before birth, and presented life on earth as a continuation of life in heaven.

I have already said on another occasion, and from another point of view, that on the whole our time no longer has the kind of awareness that belonged to those times. We have a word we use to express that death is not the end of life, the word 'immortality', deathlessness. We do not have a word to express that the beginning of an earth life is not the beginning of life altogether. There is no word similar to 'immortality' that refers to the time before birth. We ought to have the term 'unbornness'. If we had that word, and if it were as alive to us as the word 'immortality', we would be able to enter into the state of soul that people had in the ancient Orient.

If you were to put yourself in the state of soul of someone living in the ancient Orient you would be able to say: For him, life on earth did not merit much attention, for it was merely an image of life in the realm of the spirit. Nor did the people of the ancient Orient take themselves very seriously as physical human beings. The human being walking around on this earth was merely the image of a heavenly human being and it was this which largely occupied people's minds. The eternal aspect of the human being was a fact that was immediately apparent to those orientals, for it came to them as an illumination, as I have said. In daytime life, during their waking hours, they had the memory of their night-time life. To gain a mental image of such a state of soul we have to go back to the ancient Orient.

The great culture of the ancient Orient goes back to far distant times. Any of it still to be found in books, even in the glorious Veda, in Vedanta philosophy, is merely a faint echo. To see the contents of that ancient oriental wisdom in their pure original form we would have to go a long way back to a much earlier period than that of the Veda. This can only be done with the aid of spiritual science. In that ancient oriental culture the whole of life on earth was illumined by insight into the spiritual world—an insight that, whilst it may have been instinctive, was also sublime. This culture then fell into decadence. If you take a good look at oriental culture as it essentially is today you will find that the underlying impulse is still to focus attention on the divine human being. Echoes of this underlying trend are to be found even in Rabindranath Tagore's superficialities. Tagore is entirely immersed in a later, decadent culture but, as I said, the underlying trend is still there in his writings, which in part are of tremendous interest and significance, though basically completely superficial. An example are the essays collected in his book on nationalism.[62] When we look to the Orient, therefore, we see an ancient, sublime, instinctive culture with a marked emphasis on life before birth. And we also see the gradual decline of what originally was a sublime culture. The decline reveals an inability to take up the mission of modern humanity, to enter properly into the existence we have between birth and death. In ancient times the people of the Orient were given the ideal image of the human being. They saw life in the physical, sense-perceptible world as a reflection of that ideal. This heavenly and divine ideal had been full of life and luminosity. Gradually it darkened and became obscured and all that was left was a shadow image. By now it has faded completely. A shadow image remained of something that once presented itself to the soul as alight and alive, the ideal image the human being had of himself as soul and spirit, part of a whole cosmos of soul and spirit.

A certain impotence also formed part of oriental nature. This is something of which we must take special note if we want to live in accord with our age. Orientals were left with a certain inability to observe the human being whose image is perceived during the time between birth and death. Orientals had no real interest in this in the past, not even when what they came face to face with was not a substitute but something quite different—a human being who was both heavenly and physical. Even today they are not really interested in human beings the way they are between birth and death. It was left to another culture to consider the true nature of the human being here in the world of the senses between birth and death. It was left to a culture which I should like to call the culture of the Middle. Historically this culture of the Middle first appeared during the latter part of the ancient Greek period. Original Greek antiquity still echoed ancient oriental wisdom. Later the element began to appear which I am now going to characterize as the culture of the 'Middle' or the 'Centre'.

The culture of the Middle came up from a southerly direction and spread through the late Greek and then, particularly, the Roman world. Vision was the characteristic of the oriental culture I have described. The element that came up from the south, spreading through the late Greek world and assuming its true form in the Roman world—finally becoming the culture of Middle—came to be a culture based on law, dialectics and intellectual thinking. It came to be a culture not of visionaries but of thinkers. This intellectual culture has a particular capacity for considering the human being between birth and death. It went through preliminary stages in the late Greek period, grew tough and indeed brutal in the Roman Empire, and was kept alive in the language of ancient Rome; the Latin language, the language used by scientists right into the Middle Ages. This dialectical and intellectual culture reached its high point at the turn of the 18th to the 19th century. That was the time of Schiller, Goethe, Herder and also the philosophers Fichte, Schelling and Hegel. Consider the characteristic nature of those great minds and you will see that I am right in what I am saying.

Take Fichte, Schelling, even Goethe. What made them great? Their greatness and significance has to do with perception of the human being between birth and death. They demanded that the human being must be perceived and understood as a whole. Take Hegelian philosophy, for example. You will find that great emphasis is put on the spiritual nature of the human being. The spirit is however only considered in so far as the human being lives between birth and death. Hegel never considered the pre-birth existence of a heavenly and divine human being. He presented a historical approach to everything that happened among human beings here on earth, always in so far as they were human beings living between birth and death. You will find nothing about the intervention of powers from the world in which human beings live between death and rebirth. It is as if all this had been erased from that great culture, for its mission was to emphasize very clearly that here, in the life between birth and death, human beings have soul and spirit as well as a physical body. That culture had its limits, however, in that it was not possible to look up to a life in the spirit. The soul principle that goes beyond birth and death, the eternal element, was given tremendous emphasis particularly by Hegel, but also by all other great thinkers, especially in Germany. Yet they only took account of it in so far as it came to revelation between birth and death; they completely lacked the ability to see into life eternal as it comes to revelation before birth and again after death. When people spoke of a human being independent of the body, they were using an original tradition that had not welled up from their own perception. It was mere tradition. In the intellectual life of Central Europe at that time, tremendous perceptive powers had been developed that focused on the soul and spirit of human beings, but at the same time also on their physical bodies. These tremendous powers did not however extend beyond the life between birth and death.

In the West all kinds of new beginnings were emerging for a different kind of life that will evolve in times to come, when a spiritual principle that is free of the body will come into life in a different way. Let us recall—how did the people of the ancient Orient let the spiritual element enter into their lives? They remembered in the daytime the things they had experienced at night, when they had been outside their bodies, between going to sleep and waking up. This will be different in times to come. Today we have merely the early signs, the preliminary stages of this. Between waking up and going to sleep human beings do not merely have experience of the things of which they are conscious. Little of what we actually experience is at present coming to conscious awareness. The truth is that down below in our human nature we experience immeasurably more than we are able to hold in awareness. Some people already have an idea of this, particularly in the West. Thus William James[63] was speaking of a 'subconscious' or 'unconscious' because he had an inkling of this, but none of these people have so far been able to achieve full insight. Everything said on the subject is like the babbling of infants, but the idea is there. In the ancient Orient experience of the cosmic soul and spirit entered into awareness that had been gained when free of the body. The time will come when the unconscious contents—experienced in the depth of human nature—will rise up into awareness for the people of the Western world. Imaginations will also arise. Association psychology as it is practised today is a nonsense, but anyone who has studied the different psychologies of the Western world, today, can see that it is a preparatory stage.

In time to come something that came to the people of the Middle only as a revelation of human experience between birth and death, will reveal its eternal aspect through the special faculties developed in the West.

Down below we have the element that will live in the spiritual world after death. Remember what I have told you about these things on different occasions and from different points of view. I have said that the human head is the outcome of the previous life on earth. The other parts of the human being will be the head in the next life on earth. Those other parts of the human being may be flesh and blood, muscle, skin and bone as we see them today, but in essence they contain the germ of what will be the head during the next incarnation. They therefore relate to the time after death. This connection with the time after death will be revealed and brought to conscious awareness in the humanity of the future. The early, primitive stages of such a humanity are already present in the West. In future the inner soul and spirit will be imaginatively perceived, just as the soul and spirit in the world outside human beings were perceived at an instinctively imaginative level in prehistoric times. The difference will be that the revelation of these inner aspects will come to full awareness, whereas the people of the ancient Orient received revelations that were more instinctive and came only dimly to awareness.

What are the early signs to be seen today? The first signs are that in these Western regions people are very much inclined towards materialism. In time to come, the spirit will be revealed out of physical human substance. Because of this the Western world is tending to become extremely materialistic. That is the source of the materialism that is predominantly a Western product and, coming from the West, has overrun the Middle and is spreading to the East.

The culture of the Middle is not materialistic by nature. We might call it physical *and* spiritual, because the view taken of the nature of the human being is such that a balance is maintained between turning the eye to the physical aspect and turning it to the spiritual aspect. German philosophers, Goethe and Schiller have always given equal validity to body and spirit, as it were. In the West the spirit is a matter for the future; at present attention focuses on the body. Yet everything is in a state of flux in human evolution and this understanding of the body, this materialism, will one day become spiritualism. Only this spiritualism will have quite a different source than the spiritualism of the ancient Orient, and above all it will be conscious.

So you see the peculiar distribution of the three different human configurations over the world—I have discussed other aspects of this before. In the East, human beings once saw their own heavenly and spiritual image in themselves. In the Middle, human beings see themselves as inhabitants of the earth endowed with soul and spirit as well as a physical body. In the West today, human beings see themselves as merely physical; it is to be their mission, however, to develop faculties out of this physical human body that will be the spiritual content of human awareness in time to come. The early signs of this are already apparent.

The human beings of the Middle are held as in a vice between East and West. The East originally had a very advanced culture but it has fallen into decadence. In the West a great culture is to come, and the first signs are there, but at present people are still entirely caught up in the material world. In the Middle a culture has evolved that, I think I can say, holds the balance between the two. On the one hand we have the clear dialectical thinking of Schiller's letters on aesthetic education, for instance. This way of thinking goes to a point where it does not yet become subject to the superficiality of modern science but still retains a personal human element. On the other hand we have pictures of human social life like those in Goethe's *Fairy Tale of the Green Snake and the Beautiful Lily*.[64] This approach does achieve pictures or images, but it does not take them to a point where they become perceptions.

The people of the Middle have therefore also been given the mission to take the insights that their particular faculties have given them into the nature of the human being between birth and death, and to extend them through direct perception. The human being is thus seen as soul and spirit as well as a physical body, but this is then extended by immediately ascending to the wisdom of the mysteries. By developing the same faculties that have rescued soul and spirit, accepting their existence as well as that of the physical body, and by letting clear thinking develop into Imagination, Inspiration and Intuition, human beings rise again to the spiritual world in which they live between death and rebirth. Here in the physical world we will only come to experience the total illumination those faculties can give, once they have been developed, if we consider the problem of freedom. In my *Philosophy of Freedom* I have therefore concentrated entirely on that particular problem. There it was of course necessary to use this faculty, though merely to deal with earthly problems. If it is developed further, however, it will raise our horizons to include the world that lies beyond birth and death.

You see that in a sense the world also shows three stages of evolution: in the ancient Orient an instinctive wisdom, in the Middle a certain dialectical and intellectual life, and in the West today still materialism with the spiritualism of the future to be born out of it.

In the ancient Orient everything depended on that instinctive wisdom. Political life as we know it did not yet exist. The people who presided over the mysteries also set the tone for political and economic life. Greatness for the people of the ancient Orient lay in life of the spirit that developed instinctively. Political and economic life depended on this life in the spirit. The life style of the European Middle did, of course, originally come from the South; its first beginnings go back as far as Egypt. The life style that evolved in the Middle reached the point where the state, the political element, was thought through dialectically. Political life—the state—really developed in this culture of the Middle. The life of the spirit became mere tradition. In the West, finally, in Puritanism, for instance, the spiritual element became something entirely abstract, something that could become sectarian, and people let this illumine their ordinary everyday physical lives.

The European Middle therefore provided the soil where above all political ideas were developed further by Wilhelm von Humboldt[65] for instance and even took such marvellous form as the 'social community' in Schiller's letters on aesthetic education. They were presented to human minds in the grandiose pictures created by Goethe; his *'Tale' of the Green Snake and the Beautiful Lily* basically presents the idea of the state.

In the West, ideas that have so far developed only in relation to material things, to economics, will one day have to evolve into the threefold social order. The idea of the state has merely been inherited from the culture of the Middle. Woodrow Wilson, who used to be very famous, has written a large volume on the subject of the state.[66] This contains nothing that has originated in the West; all it does is repeat the theories relating to the body politic that have been developed in the Middle, including specific ideas. The book has even been translated into German, because in Germany, too, Woodrow Wilson was considered a great man for a time.

It may therefore be said that the idea of a threefold social organism which is present in our minds has evolved in three historial stages. In the ancient Orient instinctive ideals became the life of the spirit. The culture of the Middle was partly instinctive—the idea of the state developed by Humboldt, Schiller, Herder and others who were to follow is half instinctive and half intellectual—with the emphasis on the sphere of rights and on political life. Economic life, as such, really is in the first instance the business of the West. It is the business of the West to such an extent that even the philosophers of the West are really out-of-place economists. Spencer would have done a great deal better to have established factories, rather than philosophies. The specific configuration of the West really fits the structure of a factory. There you will find all all the things that Spencer was considering.

There is also another way of putting it: In the ancient Orient human beings ascended to the divine aspect of man. For them, man was in a way the son of the deity, the issue of the divine principle. The divine was in a way reaching down, as the ancient orientals saw it. It had a downward extension that was then merely reproduced: the human being on earth was a continuation of the divine model. They saw the divine and spiritual human being above, and the physical human being—as the image of that divine being—in the world below. They merely saw something of the heavenly human being hanging down, as it were, reaching down into the physical world. Later the heavenly human being came to be forgotten, only a faint idea remained in a culture grown decadent, and people no longer had any feeling for something of the divine human being reaching down into the human being on earth.

The people of the Middle are organized in such a way that the aspect of the heavenly human being reaching down from the heights of the spirit has condensed into a kind of closed semicircle, with the physical human being joined on to this. A being of divine spirit and physical, bodily nature, a being the mind could entirely encompass, was the result. This is beautifully shown in Hegel's philosophy and Goethe had it beautifully present in his mind.

In the culture of the West attention focuses on the animal world, on animal nature. Darwin presented a magnificent view of its evolution. At the top is a kind of rounded peak. This is difficult to grasp. It is merely considered the highest product of evolution: the human being. In reality the West considers only animal nature, just as the East only considered the heavenly aspect, the god finding continuation in man. In the West attention focuses on the animal world. This comes to a rounded peak in a creature seen as a continuation of the evolutionary sequence of animals, a kind of super-animal extending beyond animal nature. That is as far as the West has got. The point which has been reached is reflected in Western philosophy. It will develop further and the people of the Occident will one day give form and substance to the spiritual element from below, just as the people of the Orient received it from above. But in the West it will be done in full conscious awareness. The Middle represents the transition between the two.

When one is considering real things it feels wrong to speak of an age of transition. Every age is one of transition of course, because there will always be something that went before and something that follows. Yet in a plant the calyx is in a definite place for instance, with the flowers above and the leaves below. One does get clear divisions. In the same way there are clear divisions in human evolution. We can certainly call the time when the great slaughter was in progress, from 1914 onwards, a time of transition, a time that stands out in the historical evolution of humankind. It also was a time when the destiny of the people of the Middle developed in a way that is full of inner tragedy in certain respects. The people of the Middle were faced with a great question: 'How do we find the way from physical life between birth and death on this earth to life between death and rebirth?' Hegel's philosophy immediately turned into materialism afterwards. The first half of the 19th century was unable to answer the question: 'How do we extend the insight we have gained into the spiritual element present here on earth to the spheres beyond this earth?' That indeed is the great question specifically facing us, the question put to the culture of the Middle. Goetheanism must be developed further. It must develop in the direction of soul and spirit. It must grow out of merely physical human concerns and become cosmic. Spiritual science working towards Anthroposophy is attempting to do this. It is a continuation of Goetheanism, extending into the spiritual realm. Goetheanism must be extended to become mystery wisdom. It has to be developed to grow into mystery wisdom.

That is the significant aspect of the signature of the present time. We must understand it before we can consciously take our place in the life of the present, in the work that has to be done at the present time. The Central European element has been severely put to the test.

If it does not falter, its task will be to deepen its perception of human existence in the physical, sense-perceptible world; a perception in which the spirit is still present in the physical, sense-perceptible world. That will have to be the basis on which a mystery wisdom is developed, using the same clear intellect as that used to gain understanding of the physical, sense-perceptible worled. The European Middle therefore must, or ought to, come to understand very clearly how a balance is achieved between the three spheres of culture, politics and the economy. The others will then simply follow suit. Here in the Middle people would be utterly remiss, however, if they refused to wake up and ignored the great necessity that has arisen—to grasp and put into effect the impulse for a threefold order of the social organism.

The European Middle is held as in a vice between East and West. Today it lies prostrate. Out of the very darkness of despair it has to find its way to the light.

In the next lecture we will talk about what is to happen before the middle of this century. I shall speak to you about the Christ appearing before the middle of the 20th century. This reappearance of the Christ is something I hinted at in my first mystery play. For the moment let me just say that this reappearance of the Christ is closely bound up with our understanding of the threefold nature of the whole of the cosmos. It will come about in so far as the Middle will have to turn its attention on the one hand to the instinctive spiritual culture of the East, a culture grown old, and on the other hand to the West. It must turn its attention to the West with a thorough understanding of what is in preparation there in a culture that is still materialistic today, but whose materialism holds the seed of a spirituality of the future. The culture of the Middle must take its place in the middle; it must find the energy and the strength to take its place there and point the way.

It causes me great pain and my heart feels sore because souls are not open today to receive the words that speak of the necessities of which I have spoken. It causes me pain that people want to stay asleep, want to let themselves go; that they shrink from the great tasks that have to be done today. We must look to the East and look to the West and understand what is in progress there.

It has to be clearly understood that Western culture is in its initial stages. We can see that this is most immediately apparent at the point where economic processes sprout from technological processes, if I may put it like this. A very typical example is the ideal once conceived by an American, an ideal that is bound to come to realization in the West one day. It is a purely ahrimanic ideal but one of high ideality. It consists of using the vibrations generated in the human organism, studying them in great detail and applying them to machines to the effect that if someone stood by a machine even his smallest vibrations would be intensified in that machine. The vibrations of human nerves would be transferred to the machine. Think of the Keely engine.[67] It did not succeed at the first attempt because it had been largely developed from instinct, but it is something that will certainly be realized one day. Here something arises from the crude mechanistic material world that points to what is to come—material mechanics linking up with immaterial, spiritual elements.

In the East, on the other hand, the old spirituality is increasingly falling into decadence, into decay. It is rotting away. The experience we have of the East is such that we may certainly say: The human being once perceived as a heavenly, spiritual being has come to look like a senile old person. This human being still has no understanding for the things of the earth, for the things in which human beings, too, are clothed on this earth. The West understands earthly things only, the East has no understanding of them. Because of this, the heavenly element has grown completely senile. It is always a great mistake not to pay proper attention to the way in which the spiritual element still has to be won from the mechanical genius, the mechanistic materialism of the West. The spirit will have to be intuitively gathered out of a science that is also still very much subject to Western materialism. In the same way it is a great mistake to cast sidelong glances at the East and to try and bring the spiritual life of the East to the West, in this day and age. The Theosophical Society based at Adyar used to do this and perhaps still does in its antiquated ways. Looking across to the East, nothing one finds there has anything in it that relates to present life; it is something grown old, and has to be studied as something historical that has grown old—something of no significance for the present.

In the West, if I may put it like this, we have Keely and his engine as a rough, crude mechanistic forerunner of a future culture. The final upshot of the East's spiritual senility on the other hand may be seen in the work of Tolstoy. There we see a concentrated form of something that has once been great and is now completely decadent. This is an interesting phenomenon but it does not have the least significance for the present. Much has been wiped out with the events that happened from 1914 onwards, and this includes that last flame of Eastern senility flickering up in Tolstoy. Before the war it was still possible to speak of Tolstoy as relating to the present time. The war has put an end to this and Tolstoy is no longer of significance. It is definitely out of date to speak of Tolstoy as though he were of significance today. And we must take care not to cast any kind of sidelong glance in the direction of the East, of the ancient East, and at the things that have in a way grown senile and come to a final concentration once again in an individual such as Tolstoy. We must take our stand on the mission that belongs to the present time. We can only do so if we grasp the impulse for a threefold order of the social organism out of what lies in ourselves. The decaying East has created a symbol, as it were, in world history—or we might say a symptom—in making Tolstoy a kind of final upshot, full of inner activity, and yet impotent. The West on the other hand has produced Keely with his engine as a first forerunner. Tolstoy showed how the old oriental culture had grown completely luciferic; Western culture is still entirely under the sign of the ahrimanic element.

This is what we must grasp in the present age. On the one hand we must be wary of past elements reaching across from the East, be wary of past elements from the East in someone living in this century and on the other hand we must be wary of what is only in its beginnings in the West. If we fail to grasp this and fail to perceive the true nature of these things we do not belong to the present age. Someone belonging to the present age may of course be English, French, American or Russian—humanity must extend beyond geographical boundaries today. It is important however to consider the old geographical limits because of their role in the historical evolution of humankind. Behind us lies a history of humankind that went in three stages—Orient, Middle, West. Before us—and this is something spiritual science working towards Anthroposophy must really stress—lies the time when we will be purely human beings, holding the East, the Middle and the West within us at one and the same time. Anyone born to be truly alive today—and this includes anyone who is Asian—is capable of holding all three within him or her. The people of the Middle need not limit themselves to holding the Middle within them. They must gain inner experience of the historical East in its decadence and the historical West which is in the ascendant. And Americans can hold East, Middle and West within themselves if they give thought to mystery wisdom— they actually need it more than most—and raise their thinking from being concerned entirely with the economy to include the spheres of politics and the life of the spirit.

That is what we must say today when we want to define the tasks which human individuals should come to realize are the tasks given to the innermost soul. We will recognize these tasks if we consider the great needs of the present age.

Stuttgart, 14 November 1920

So far a number of different approaches have been used to consider the effective forces in human evolution which we must know about if we want to arrive at a proper understanding of current events. We must above all understand where the root causes lie that have led to the disastrous situation we are facing today. Only then can we find the right way of taking effective action ourselves, and work for the real progress of humankind. Unfortunately far too little attention is paid to the changes which those forces effective in human evolution have undergone in very recent times, compared to times that relatively speaking were not that long ago.

Perhaps I may again be permitted to take the great disaster that has happened in recent years as my starting point. This will lead us to the event I referred to in just a few words at the end of my last talk, to the specific Christ event that belongs to the first half of the 20th century, as I have mentioned a number of times.

Taking a genuinely unbiased view of the disastrous events and of their consequences that continue into the present and will still make themselves felt for a long time, we cannot fail to notice how much the whole fabric of the destiny of civilized humanity differs from earlier times. Let me point out immediately that large numbers of people, including those in authority, have not yet become fully aware of what has come upon us. They have been, and still are, acting in accord with the demands of earlier times and their actions are not at all in accord with the needs of the present age.

Again let me give an example, just by way of introduction as it were. We have a—well, they call it a 'war' behind us; a much greater war than any we know of in historical times. We have seen that at the time when the war started, something like a spectre from prehistoric times lived in the thoughts that were in people's minds, and that this spectre is still there in the minds of people today. We have seen that this spectre of ideas which has continued into the present from prehistoric times has given rise to opinions, all kinds of measures were taken, and people had no idea that really and fundamentally something quite different was going on to what they imagined the events of the time to be.

Like earlier wars, the last one was a conflict between human beings; human beings were fighting each other. Unlike earlier wars, however, this war involved energies and forces coming from quite different sources than the form of energies used in earlier wars—energies deriving from the particular nature of human beings. We have seen a tremendous development of technology in recent times and the coming of this powerful technology has changed the whole situation, where the destiny fabric of human beings is concerned. This change determined the course of events in recent years. Yet there has been no corresponding change in people's ideas.

Let me present the major aspects of this. During the period preceding this disastrous war the human technology which had evolved in most recent times had reached a significant stage. Although people had no real awareness of this, human work—labour—had taken on quite a different form to what had gone before. You can get an idea of the different forms it took if you consider one of the fundamental aspects of modern technology, let us say coal-mining, in different countries in the civilized world. The amount of coal produced in the mines relates to the amount of energy gained by processing it; energies merely channelled and controlled by human beings that will then work more or less independently. I would say, therefore, that in recent times human work has come to consist more in stepping back and directing the actual work done by machines.

Considering the facts one will find, for instance, that during the period preceding the outbreak of war, 79 million 'horse power years' of that kind of energy were produced in Germany. These were energies controlled by humans, but in fact derived from coal-mining. They did not arise from something that human beings let spontaneously come forth from within them, but from completely external actions and processes. The energies expended in work are measured in units based on the work a horse does in a year. During the time immediately preceding the outbreak of war, Germany was producing 79 million horse power years of coal-derived energy per year.

What does this really mean? A very superficial comparison with the population figure for Germany shows that on average every single individual in Germany had a horse by his side. This means that the inhabitants of Germany did so much work in the field of technology that is was equivalent to every individual having a horse work for him all year long. The population figure was approximately 79 million, and the energy used was 79 million horse power years. The work done by machines, all kinds of machines, therefore had the same effect as if every individual had a horse to work for him. When war broke out, the potential was there for that much work to be done. A large proportion of this work was then used for the purposes of war, with the result that the purely technological effect of 79 million horse power years was brought into action at the front.

Now let us take some other figures. For a start I will just add the fact that in 1870, a year when another great event[68] took place the way people see it—and rightly so, as people see it—no 79 million horse power years were produced. Energy production was then six whole millions and seven-tenths of a million, a very low figure compared to human energy output. Six and a half million in 1870, 79 million in 1912. Clearly this means a complete change in the human situation.

Let me give you some more figures. During the time preceding the disastrous war, France, Russia and Belgium together had 35 million horse power years available. Great Britain on the other hand had 98 million. Due to the geographical position of Great Britain those 98 million horse power years could not immediately be fully brought to bear in the war zone; it took some years until this was achieved. When war broke out, therefore, not only were human beings opposing each other, but 79 million horse power years had been pushed into the front lines by the Germans, or a total of more than 90 million by the Central Powers [Germany and Austria]. A large part of those energies were of course used in the war industries and therefore reached the front lines indirectly. Those energies were opposed by Great Britain's 98 million horse power years that could only be brought to bear gradually, and a total of 35 million available in Belgium, Russia and France. You can see now that it would be quite correct to say that, basically, the contribution made by human beings only gave a preliminary result in the initial stages. The army's general staff could order the troops to march; that could be planned and projected by trained minds. But when the front lines had been established for some years, the actual confrontation was between the horse power years that technology had produced—and these were quite independent of human beings. Thus the relative size of something that had really been taken out of the sphere of human activity determined the fate of this [part of] human evolution. If you now take the following and add it to what has been already said you will see that forces independent of humanity, particularly the most recent achievements of technology, have been responsible for the events that occurred.

The efforts of human beings were of course limited to a channelling function, or at best to stopping some things from happening. But their directions, or else their failure to stop things from happening, caused forces to enter the field of battle that objectively speaking were not under their control. Some of these were able to overcome the others, as it were, on the basis of objective laws that had nothing to do with human beings. Add to this the fact that the United States intervened in the process. At the time when the other countries were able to field the number of horse power years I have mentioned, the Americans were in a position to mobilize 179 million horse power years. This gives you the relative figures for energies mobilized through technology; energies completely independent of anything human beings are capable of producing. Indirectly they are of course connected with ideas thought up by human individuals and so on. The things people have thought up have however been channelled in this direction, and in the war the situation then was that objective force met objective force and in the final instance this had to decide the issue. In very recent times human beings directed their destinies to such effect that when something occurred that in the past would have taken quite a different course, human actions had caused the forces of destiny to be surrendered to the powers that were active in the objects they themselves had produced. Humans are dependent on the earth's productivity where these forces are concerned. They are dependent on many factors that do not lie within their own skins.

This reveals one of the characteristic features of the present age. I have merely given the most striking example of it. Examples like this can be used to illustrate a point. Yet the things that happened there on a gigantic scale—we cannot merely say on a large scale, because it was gigantic—happen on a smaller scale in every day of the life we are given, for we have been delivered up to the products of technology. In 1912 a point had been reached in Germany where fertile human brains had created something outside themselves that did the same amount of work for every individual as a horse would have done. That is the characteristic feature of modern civilization, and we must take a good look at it.

What is alive in those forces with their own objective activity that human beings have created outside themselves in modern civilization; forces that work for them day by day and determine their destinies? Looking at these forces and the way they influence human destiny we perceive the power that we have come to call the power of Ahriman. Ahrimanic powers are alive in these things. Looking at it like this, you will have to admit that the power of these ahrimainc forces has increased at a tremendous rate. Just consider those two figures I have given: in 1870, six and a half million horse power years were available in Germany; that is not very much per human being. In 1912, 79 million horse power years were produced in Germany. That is the sum total of these things influencing not only economic life but the rest of our life as well. So you see what goes on in a world constructed by human beings, that is quite independent of what really lies in human nature. These forces are completely at odds with everything that came into effect when people faced each other as human beings, in the battles fought in the ancient Orient, for instance. Only luciferic forces were involved in those, and this still held true when the Tartar hordes invaded Europe, for example. We often do not realize how different the world has become for modern humanity and how quickly this has come about, relatively speaking.

Spiritual science working towards Anthroposophy is, moreover, called upon to consider the full implications of such a fact. So far I have merely described the outer aspect. We begin to see the inner aspect when we consider the powers which are active in this. In the past they were luciferic powers and now they are ahrimanic. Human beings find themselves in the middle between the two. First of all, however, we must get a definite idea as to what we mean by 'ahrimanic' and 'luciferic'.

Consider what went on in human soul life in those past times when the great struggles in which human beings were involved were largely determined by luciferic elements. At that time people looked at the phenomena in the world and, as you know, they looked at them in such a way that they perceived a certain number of elemental beings—let us say demonic spirits. Materialistic scientists call this the 'age of vitalism', saying that people introduced all kinds of water sprites, gnomes and so on into the phenomenal world. We know that spirits are indeed active in the phenomena of nature. Today, people see only dry-as-dust, prosaic natural phenomena. In the past, people perceived the spiritual entities, the essential spirit of natural phenomena. This is called superstition, nowadays. That is the view taken by the present age. We know, however, that the people of the past used those names to describe something real, which their minds perceived when they looked at the phenomena of nature. They saw elemental spirits in everything nature presented to them. Thus we may say that however instinctive, dim and dreamlike their conscious awareness may have been, some illumination was received as to the nature of those elemental spirits.

During the times that followed, perception of the spiritual essence of natural phenomena no longer came clearly to awareness when people looked at the natural world around them, that did not depend on them for its existence. The modern intellectual approach that we call a scientific attitude came into being. This only concerns itself with forces that can be abstracted from nature and made comprehensible through abstract ideas, in short, the things that may form the content of the human intellect.

I would say, however, that without people being aware of it a completely new world developed in a relatively short time—just take the time from 1870, when six and seven-tenths million horse power years were used in Germany, to 1912, when 79 million were used. This is a world that did not exist before. These forces are present in the human environment, and in major events like those we have seen in recent years. Human destiny actually depended on them, just as formerly it had depended on natural phenomena. These forces and energies also exist and take effect independent of human beings, just as the forces of nature are independent of human beings. Demons—

elemental powers—are active in them, but their effects on human beings differ from those of the elemental powers that human beings perceived in the phenoma of nature in the past. Then, people would look at the phenomena of nature and say: 'Elemental spirits are at work in there.' That had an effect on their conscious awareness; the soul came to an understanding with the phenomena of nature, and the conscious mind could relate to those phenomena. Today's 'enlightened' minds consider it superstitious to look for spiritual powers in natural phenomena. They have not the least idea that demonic spirits are active in the whole world of technology created by the human race. Nor will they find it easy to see this, because those powers are acting on the will—and I have often told you that the will is alseep. They work at an unconscious level, taking hold of the unconcious human mind. The consequence is as follows. In the past human beings had at least some awareness of demonic powers. Today demonic powers are restively stirring in all products of technology;[69] their activities extend into the sphere of the human will, but human beings are not yet inclined to accept this. In the first place these things are at an unconscious level and in the second place people feel it would be superstitious to say that demonic spirits are active in the machines they have produced. They are active nevertheless. The spirits perceived in the phenomena of nature in older times were luciferic by nature; the spirits active in machines, in all products of technology, are ahrimanic by nature. Human beings are thus surrounding themselves with an ahrimanic world that is growing completely independent of them.

You will perceive the trend in human evolution. From a luciferic world that still influences their conscious minds and there determines their destinies, human beings are drifting into an ahrimanic world. And at present this is happening at quite a fast pace. This ahrimanic world acts on the human will, and the intellectualism of modern science does not enable people to gain immediate conscious awareness of the will. The great danger is that the ahrimanic world will take hold of the human will and human beings will completely lose their bearings among the demonic powers that are present in the products of technology.

In Eastern Europe present-day thinking has led to a desire to militarize the economy and make it into a vast machine. Even human beings are trained to be like machines, with human labour made into something quite separate from the human being. Behind it lies the will to call forth will demons, for it is their sphere into which people are sliding in Eastern Europe.

The road from the luciferic to the ahrimanic sphere—yes, it has to be said that the course of human evolution is going in that direction. Fundamentally speaking we are right in the middle of leaving the luciferic and sliding into the ahrimanic sphere. Luciferic elements are of course still present in many ways. The ahrimanic element is taking hold of people. The luciferic is more alive in feelings. The ahrimanic takes effect through the human intellect and comes to realization as it takes form in the products of technology.

And now the Christ event, which we may expect during the first half of the 20th century, enters into the situation to give human beings their bearings. The nature of this Christ event will be such that more people will be having objective experiences and will then know that the etheric Christ is walking on earth, the Christ who will represent the power that once walked on earth in the physical form of Christ Jesus, but now at the etheric level. If people come to know this Christ power, if they let it enter into them, they will find the right way of dealing with the forces influencing them that come from the ahrimanic powers which are now in the ascendant. The great problem of our time is that people slide into the ahrimanic sphere without having the support of the Christ force.

We are speaking of something very concrete and positive when we refer to this event that is entering into human evolution in the 20th century. In my first mystery [play] I referred to this as the reappearance of the Christ. I would also say that it is possible to perceive what will happen in human souls when they meet this Christ event in a living way.

The other day I was able to indicate in a public lecture[70] that the scientific thinking of the West, which is totally lacking in cohesive vision, reaches its limits when it comes to perceiving the nature of the human being. Science mostly grasps the non-living world. This is categorized and so on. Theories are developed concerning both the non-living and the living world. Darwinism does not go beyond the evolution of animals, however. The human being is then placed at the top of the tree, but this theory really does not include the human being. It is unable to perceive the nature of the human being.

The same applies to the comprehension of social concepts. I have shown that people really 'run on rails' when working in this field; their approach is ahrimanic, technical, and they do not go beyond this. They have got it all down in their books, where credits and liabilities are recorded. They fail, however, to consider the people involved. Those people want their dignity as human beings to be recognized, but no bridges are built between management and workers. Practical life fails to take account of the nature of the human being.

On one side all this is still more or less theoretical today—though perhaps we should not call it theory but rather the impotence of theory, of perception. On the other side we have something that is much to the fore in the social sphere today. The things that are not written down in the books are today making themselves felt in strikes and revolutionary movements. They show themselves in life and they arise out of the work done in industry, in commerce and so on, just as much as all kinds of goods result from industrial production. It is merely that this element, which is now causing unrest among the people, had not been included in the textbooks. It is therefore making itself felt in real life.

I believe it is true to say that very few people really think about these things—which I also discussed at that recent public lecture. The 19th century has really been clouding the issue where these matters are concerned. During the 18th century some people, certainly the more radical thinkers, did begin to get an idea as to what was coming. The 19th century brought events which caused grand-scale confusion. Pierre Bayle[71] made a very peculiar statement in the 18th century. He was one of the 18th-century materialists who were the forerunners of 19th-century materialism. His statement went as follows: 'States will know honour and dishonour, ambition, egotism and so forth, but there cannot be a state in which Christian attitudes play an effective role; it is possible to have a state system in which the old heathen virtues and vices play a role, but there can be no such a thing as a Christian state.' Those were the words of Pierre Bayle, a radical materialist, and there was more truth to his words than to those of the 19th-century idealists. Those idealistic thinkers pretended to themselves that states were Christian. The truth is that they were not. Consider the Christian beliefs of the Middle Ages, for those were foremost in Pierre Bayle's mind. Those beliefs were based on a denial of this earth. It was considered a virtue to rise to a life that was not of this world. The life that developed during the 18th century was largely concerned with earthly matters. 'There can be no such thing as a Christian state', Pierre Bayle said, and that in fact was the truth. People were lying when, in the 19th and early 20th century, they pretended to themselves and others that the modern states which had gradually evolved had the Christ spirit in them. They cannot be Christian. Something else emerged from this, however. Whether they stood in the pulpit, or heard the words that were spoken from the pulpit, people felt utterly convinced that they were true Christians. In the same way people going to their work in government offices, putting on their medals or using the titles conferred on them by the state, imagined themselves to be Christian. They were not in fact Christians, for they held those very positions on account of the fact that they were not Christians. People got into the habit of living a lie; they got out of the habit of seeing the truth when it came to major aspects of life. The result was a nebulous atmosphere where it was not even possible to develop an unbiased view of the progressive ahrimanization of the world.

There has been a lot of talk about the campaign of lies we have had in recent years. Yet in all most important respects people have actually got used to such campaigns of lies. What reason is there to tell the truth now about the lies that were told during that disastrous war? After all, during the 19th century people got into a habit where their souls no longer wanted to know the truth, when it came to the things that are most important in their lives.

It is uncomfortable to face up to these things, and the problem is that people are not facing up to them. Apart from anything else, therefore, modern people are in the difficult position that has arisen because of their inner untruthfulness. This atmosphere will cause a particular mood to develop. Until now it has been mere theory in many respects, merely something we know, that human beings can no longer get through to each other; that the nature of the human being cannot be understood and that this failure to get through to others is also having an effect in the social sphere. All this will become deposited on the human soul. The influence of the external products of technology on the will is going to make the unconscious react with the conscious sphere. There will be no conscious awareness of this, of course, for the whole is at a subconscious level, but a mood will be created. This mood will emerge more and more over the next few decades, or rather years, taking hold of large numbers of people. You will be teaching children in your school and you will note that these children come up with feelings that their elders never had. Something like this has also existed in earlier ages, but it will happen to a much greater degree in the near future. Profound spiritual insight into the present age will be able to judge what is evolving from the depths of the souls of these young people. A great longing is going to come, a kind of longing for something that is lacking. Initially, theories could not be developed that embraced the true nature of the human being, and in the social sphere it proved impossible to include human gifts and talents in business ledgers. All this will condense into feelings and emotions. There will be people—we shall find them among the young in the next generations—who will feel like this: 'Well, here I am. My form is different from that of other life forms around me. I do not look like an animal, an ox, a donkey, a weasel or an eagle. I look different, but I do not know what it is that looks different. I do not know what a human being is; I do not know what I am.' Despondency and neurosis will invade the souls of the coming generation. This will be the mood of the age that teachers perceive when they give their lessons. It will be a mood that spreads far and wide. People are so superficial nowadays that is is difficult to talk to them about these things. To show what I mean let me remind you that during the 18th century people who had some perception of the soul of that age were speaking of a 'Werther fever'. Goethe wrote his *Werther*[72] out of the whole mood of that age. Then another novel called *Siegwart*[73] appeared. This had been written out of the 'Siegwart fever' of the second half of the 18th century. Those were the moods of the times, but they only affected a limited number of people. A mood will however arise in the souls of vast numbers of people that may be brought to expression as follows: 'Well, what am I as a human being? What kind of life form am I as I walk around on two legs? I have a science that I have taken to great heights; I have a life in the social sphere—yet both of them do not touch on the reality of what I am.' This mood will be the great question mark of the age, a question mark as to one's own nature as a human being. It will prepare the eye of the soul so that it may perceive something that is difficult to describe but will nevertheless come to be the new Christ event. Out of that longing, the power will arise to see the Christ made evident. Outer want will become an inner want for the soul, and out of this inner want is to be born the vision of the Christ who will be walking unseen among human beings, and they will need to hold on to him to stop them from sliding from the luciferic into the ahrimanic sphere, in a way that is quite unthinkable.

What good is the whole of science to us if it cannot help us get a really concrete grasp of human life in its immediacy? It has to be clearly understood that human beings as they are today already have a whole number of earth lives behind them. We live through repeated earth lives. In earlier earth lives we ourselves have seen elemental powers at work in the phenomena of nature. We have brought the fruits of those earlier earth lives into our present life. Then, we knew that nature spirits around us determined our destinies, and that we had those spirits within us. Today we consider nature entirely with the intellect, with the head, and the products of technology we ourselves have produced are considered in the same way. All we see are the contents of our intellect. But out of the many earth lives we have lived through—though we refuse to consider them nowadays—something is restlessly astir in us that I have called a great longing, a longing for something that is lacking. We have been human beings who looked at nature and saw the spirit; this enabled us to develop an inner feeling for the true nature of human beings. Now we have a science and a social awareness that do not get as far as the human being. Our past vision of the world around us has given us the potential capacity to feel ourselves to be human beings. Today we look into a nature empty of human beings, we do not penetrate as far as the human being. This will create a great need in the souls of people in the decades to come. This need in the souls of people is a positive power, and out of this positive power will be born the ability to see the Christ.

The old way of approaching the Christ has been destroyed by the theology of most recent times. Our modern theology has made the Christ into the 'simple man of Nazareth'. Surely it will be impossible for human beings to relate to the Christ event today unless there is a renewal of life in the spirit.

The Catholic Church knew very well why it did not want the masses to have direct access to the Gospels. In theory, catholics are still not permitted to read the Gospels. The Albigenses, Waldenses and others who would not accept this were, of course, declared heretics because the church was only too well aware what would happen if the Gospels became accessible to the masses. In the first place there are four Gospels. The divine spirit reveals itself to humankind in those four forms. You cannot, however, use the intellect to present an event in four different ways the way it has been done in the Gospels, for then contradictions, will arise. The moment you deny the Gospels their reality, considering them to be the products of the human intellect, they inevitably become contradictory, full of contradictions. What has emerged, therefore, is the total destruction of any way in which the Mystery of Golgotha may be perceived.

Again people live with the lie that they are supposed to be Christians, and yet the source has been blocked and brought to nought because modern theology no longer has anything in it that is Christian. To regain Christianity we must acquire a new spiritual vision. Access has to be again gained to the treasure we have gathered in our souls, a treasure we have carried with us through many earth lives.

Our present life, the life we now find ourselves in, is also the starting point for future earth lives. The abstract thinking we use for mathematics, and the various moods of which the soul has concrete experience, are the inheritance of earlier earth lives. Everything we take in of the outside world in this earth life will provide the germ for faculties we shall have in future earth lives. In the past, people came to see elemental spirits active in the world of nature outside. When we were on earth before we looked at nature and gained an impression of elemental spirits; this is now part of us. Today life is largely determined by what the 'horse' beside us is producing, by technical things. This enters into us. Unless we do something about it this will form the basis for future earth lives in us. New demons, the ahrimanic demons, are active in it. What a way of preparing oneself for future earth lives—to allow ahrimanic powers to take over! Machines create something in us that will be the economic life in future earth lives. The roar of cannon fire at the front is something we make part of ourselves, for it is something that was alive in those machines. And so it really is our intention to be quite unconscious when we rise again in our next earth life. But human beings are more than just intellect; they also have feelings and sensibilities. These have to cope with everything entering the soul from the products of technology, from machines.

There arises yet another feeling, one I have not yet described. I was speaking of the longing for something that is lacking. At the unconscious level the soul creates something out of the products of technology, out of the ahrimanic powers, and this acts into higher levels, entering our awareness in form of thoughts and ideas. Yet it arises in a form similar to fear. You will find that children you teach at school in the years and decades ahead will show this longing for something that is lacking, and also an indefinite but nevertheless tangible fear of life. This will show itself as a form of nervousness, in a nervy, fidgety character—you will find this very obvious. The first signs of it are already to be seen today.

The only way to counteract this is to fill your soul with the one thing that will give strength, a strength the earth itself cannot provide. This is the strength that has come to the earth from outside through the essential Christ who is about to appear again. It is a power we cannot gain from the earth. The earth provides technical power, the 79 million horses by our side. We must develop in our souls the strength that comes from the Christ. Otherwise we shall be filled with nothing but the power provided by the products of technology in our next life. The only cure for the nervousness that must show itself in the growing generation is to prepare ourselves for the Christ event that is to come in the first half of the 20th century.

Our age should not be described by the way it presents itself on the outside. We ought to base our description on the feelings that are paramount in human souls. It would be magnificent and important to say of our age that human beings developed an eye for what is alive in human beings. As a rule only external aspects are described. People like Paquet[74], for example—a writer who has been travelling in Eastern Europe—are in no position to give a true picture of what goes on in the hearts and minds of people who are already experiencing a great deal of the future; all such writers can do is describe things from the outside.

If spiritual science is to come alive in us it must be able to provide us with insight into the sphere of feelings and sensibilities. You do not know what life really is if you use abstract terms to speak of the Christ event that is to come; you only know what life really is if you speak of human souls moving ahead to meet this Christ event, partly with longing in their heart and partly with fear.

Surely it must be impossible for people, as they are today, to grasp such things as the way the fate of that disastrous war was sealed by ahrimanic forces quite independent of anything human beings were able to do? It was entirely determined by elements thought up in human brains that then became objective forces. It is impossible for modern people to get the right picture and assess the real effects of these things—unless they take account of spiritual science. Just think what it means that there were 79 million horse power years produced in Germany, 98 million in Great Britain, 35 million in Belgium, France and Russia, and finally the 179 million produced in the United States were added to this! We are speaking of something that takes no account of human nature, and those are the factors that truly determine human destiny today. Human beings have totally given themselves over to something that is no longer human. The statement that human insight does not go as far as the human being, now appears in a new light. Human beings remain limited to the non-human realm, even in the social sphere they will be limited to non-human aspects, unless they find the bridge that leads to the nature of the human being. That is how they fulfil their destiny today. They make their destiny partly dependent on elements that are no longer human; they produce elements which will partly determine human destiny, and yet human beings themselves will no longer be able to influence these elements. We ought no longer to be speaking of courage, of the brilliance of the general staff and the like when we want to speak of the way destinies are determined, but of the ratio of horse power years produced in different countries. Human destiny has to be discussed without reference to human beings. People will need tremendous strength to rise and face this human destiny which is determined by non-human elements and to call out: 'The destiny of the human race must be determined by human beings again!' That can only happen, of course, if people let the power of Christ enter into them. This power of Christ is approaching and it will restore them to their human powers. We can only become sure of ourselves as human beings if we walk the road created by the whole of technology, but do not let our lives be governed by the products of technology, and grow able to behold the Christ power that can become part of us and overcome all those products of technology.

These are the lessons to be learned today. These are the words that tell us how we can prepare ourselves for the Christ event. All the mediocre stuff that makes up the bulk of modern literature, all the empty talk one hears nowadays, will not help humanity to progress; it will only mean regression. Progress can solely and only be achieved with the things we gain by going down to the spiritual bedrock. And we will make no progress at all unless we become fully aware again of the seriousness of these things. It is necessary for us to understand that humanity has created a completely new world around itself today; human beings themselves have developed the energies and forces that now determine their destinies. This certainly does not merely mean the events of war. Step outside and you will see the factories that determine our destiny, and the same principle is to be found in ordinary life; it is not limited to the destinies of 1914. Ahrimanic forces are producing those smoking chimneys. The human being no longer counts there.

Walking on past the factroy we come to the church. The church still has it traditional message but this has grown abstract. It no longer has relevance in ordinary life. The church concerns itself with things that have no application in practical life. All this is luciferic, just as the things that go on in factories are ahrimanic.

The dreadful thing connected with the destiny of modern humankind is that in the places where people speak of the things of the spirit all ability has been lost to relate to real life. In a public lecture I recently gave[75] I spoke of American preachers coming to Switzerland and other neutral countries and saying something like this: 'The League of Nations must be created, for it will be a great blessing for humankind; but it cannot develop from the ideas of statesmen. It will be necessary to win people's hearts instead, so that they will believe in the League of Nations.' Anyone with an unprejudiced mind will realize that these gentlemen make very fine speeches; yet if that is enough to please us, and we find it sufficient to praise the beauty of those speeches, we fail to understand the signs of the times. Those may be honeyed words, but their sweetness does not penetrate to the hearts of the people. Those hearts are full of worry about the economic situation, and no bridge exists to words that take their origin in old religious persuasions. You cannot use them to create a League of Nations, nor can you do so with the words uttered by Woodrow Wilson,[66] Clemenceau[76] and others. What matters today is that the two must be brought together, life must be imbued with spirit, and life must be taken forward to connect with the spirit. The Christ spirit from outside the earth entered into the flesh in Jesus, a human being, uniting itself with the physical world. The Christ who will be coming during the first half of the 20th century will not use the language of abstract religious confessions—oh no! He will use the language of everyday life. People who are all the time merely looking to unearthly mystical heights for moral uplift will not understand this language. The Christ will however be speaking of the spirit even when He is speaking about everyday life. The spirit will unite with everyday life in the same way as the Christ spirit came from spheres beyond this world, beyond the world of the senses, and united with the physical human being Jesus. Such is the new understanding we must gain for the Christ event; otherwise we shall not be able to appreciate its true value when it comes upon humankind.

A question we may ask even now is the following: 'What will be the attitude of the people who are preaching official Christianity to the Christ event when it occurs during the first half of the 20th century?' If we understand the Gospels rightly, they actually provide an example for us. The Gospels speak of 'scribes and Pharisees'. Our judgement would be wrong if we were to place Adolf Harnack[77] among those who testify for the Christ; we only judge him rightly if we follow the example of the Gospels and place him among the scribes and Pharisees. And there are others of the same kind who must also be counted among them. It is essential to judge these things in the right way. We must get to the truth! The materialist Pierre Bayle said that a state could not be Christian, that states might know honour and dishonour, ambition and egotism, but that a Christian state was an impossibility. A social community in the name of Christ will however be possible, providing we do not insist on a political state but rather establish an independent life of the spirit. That can be Christian through and through. And this independent life of the spirit will be able to illumine the sphere of life where we have government and states, a sphere that simply cannot be Christian. The result will be that an economic life based on associations can develop; though this, too, cannot be Christian in itself. The people who are involved in it will be Christian, however. They will be filled with the Christ impulse. What we must do is to let people enter into an independent life of the spirit. Then it will be possible to make the whole of social life Christian.

First of all we must have truth, however. We shall not prosper with lies. These are the things we must come to accept today, inscribing them deeply in our hearts. If we fail to do so we will be siding with the people who follow Spengler[41] and believe that we have to become barbarians. Yet it also will not help if we make the facile statement that Spengler is wrong. We would simply be lying to ourselves. We will only base ourselves on the truth if we say: 'The power has to be produced that will get us forward. This, however, can only be produced out of the living spirit, out of the spirit which spiritual science working towards Anthroposophy is seeking. Spiritual science has something that must enter into the impulses of the present age if we are to have a life of the spirit that is Christian again, a political life that once again is human and does not fail to encompass the human being, and an economic life that is controlled by human beings and not by horse power years. Those horse power years that human beings have at their side are an expression of the principle which governs destiny through the products of technology, through something that is outside human beings—something inhuman.

The events of recent years cannot be read as being due to human feelings and emotions. We must read the writing of the horse power years produced by technology, the terrible signs Ahriman is beginning to write into the evolution of humankind. A new understanding of the Christ must be found so that humanity may be led out of this situation.

Stuttgart, 22 November 1920

Let us recall a number of things that are already quite familiar and use them as a starting point for important considerations. In a sense these will continue the theme I discussed some days ago.

We know that there are four major aspects to the human being and that human beings may be characterized as possessing a physical body, a life body, an astral or sentient body, and an ego. We also know that we can only really understand human beings if we add other aspects to these four. Essentially the first four refer to aspects that are fully developed at the present time. Three more have to be added—the spirit-self, the life-spirit, and the spirit-man. We know, however, that these three aspects of human nature are such that we cannot consider them to be fully developed at the present time. We can merely refer to them as future potentials inherent in human beings.

We may say that we now have a physical body and so forth, going as far as the ego, and that in time to come we shall have a spirit-self, a life-spirit and a spirit-man. We know from the anthroposophical literature that is already available that those different aspects of the human being are connected with the whole cosmos and with cosmic evolution. In a sense we relate the physical body to the earliest embodiment of this earth, which we call Ancient Saturn. The life body relates to the Ancient Sun, the astral body to the Ancient Moon, and the principle we call our I or ego relates essentially to the earth as it is at present.

What do we mean when we say that we relate to the ego we bear to the present earth? It means that inherent in the elements of the earth, the forces of the earth that are known to us—or perhaps not known to us—is the priciple that activates the ego. Our ego is intimately bound up with the forces of the earth.

If you consider the whole evolution of the human being you will find that human nature as we know it today relates largely to the past— the physical body to a far distant past, to Ancient Saturn, the life body to the time of the Ancient Sun, and so forth, and that our ego is not yet fully developed but in its esstential nature relates to the present earth. This immediately suggests that the elements we refer to as spirit-self, life-spirit and spirit-man do not in fact have their basis in the earthly realm. As human beings we have the potential to evolve into spirit-man, life-spirit and spirit-self, and this means that we have something in us that needs to be developed to go beyond this earthly realm; we will have to develop it without taking the earthly realm as our guide. As human beings we are part of this earth and our mission is in the first place to achieve full ego development; to some extent we have already developed it. The forces of the earth, the intrinsic nature of the earth, served as our guide in developing the ego to the extent to which we have now developed it. We shall continue with this development for the rest of Earth evolution, deepening and to some extent enhancing what has developed so far, and for this we shall be indebted to the earth and its forces. Yet we also have to say to ourselves that if we were entirely dependent on the earth and its forces in developing our essential human nature, we would never be able to develop a spirit-man, a life-spirit and a spirit-self. The earth has nothing to give in that respect; it is only able to help us develop the ego. With reference to human nature, therefore, the earth must be seen as something that cannot in itself make us into full human beings. We are on this earth and we have to go beyond it. Anthroposophical literature makes reference to this by showing that our evolution depends on the earth being succeeded by Jupiter, Venus and Vulcan periods. During those periods we will have to achieve full development of the spirit-self, life-spirit- and spirit-man also in outer terms.

At present, however, we are on this earth. We have to develop on this earth. The earth cannot give us everything we need to develop, in order that in future times we may progress to spirit-self, life-spirit and spirit-man. If we had to depend on the earth for everything we have to develop in ourselves we would have to do without spirit-self, life-spirit-and spirit-man.

It is easy to say such things in theory, but it is not enough to put such thoughts forward as mere theories. They will only really touch us as human beings if we allow them to take hold of the whole human being; if we come to feel the whole weight and burden of the riddle which lies in our having to say to ourselves: 'As human beings we are on this earth. We look around us. None of the many things the earth has to give—its beauty and its ugliness, its pain and suffering—none of the ways in which it can shape our destiny can provide what we need to become full human being.' There must be a longing in us that goes beyond anything the earth can give. This is something we must feel, something that must bring light and warmth into all the ideals we are capable of holding. We must be able to ask ourselves in all seriousness and very profoundly: 'What shall we do, seeing that we have only the earth around us, and yet must progress to something for which this earth cannot serve as a guide?' We must be able to experience, to feel, the full gravity of this question. In a sense we should already be able to say to ourselves that the earth is not enough for our needs, and that as human beings we will have to grow beyond this earthly realm.

Anthroposophy will be only be able to serve human beings rightly if they are able to ask themselves questions like these and really feel it; if they are aware of the gravity of such inner questions of destiny. Being aware of their gravity we can be guided in the right way to return to the Mystery of Golgotha, that has been so much part of the last two talks we have had. We may be guided back to the Mystery of Golgotha and we may be guided to consider again the event that is to happen in this century, during the first half of the 20th century, and will be like a spiritualized Mystery of Golgotha. Whenever the Mystery of Golgotha was discussed it had to be stressed that the Christ is definitely not of the earth and that the Chirst entered into an earthly body from spheres beyond this earth—doing so at exactly the right moment, as it were. In the Christ something united with this earth that came from outside, from beyond this earth. If we really experience the Christ we are able to join our own essential nature to this principle from beyond the earth, and in this way gain an energy principle; a principle that will give inner strength, filling us with inner warmth and light. This will take us beyond the earthly realm because it has not itself originated in that realm; because the Christ has come to earth from spheres beyond the earth.

We look with longing to the spheres beyond this earth because we have to say to ourselves: Longing to become complete human beings—to develop the spirit-self, life-spirit and spirit-man which we shall have to develop in the future—we survey the earth and say to ourselves that the earthly realm itself does not contain what we need to develop our own nature and take it beyond the earth. We must turn our eyes away from the earthly realm and look to the principle that has come into the earthly realm from beyond the earth. We must look to the Christ and say to ourselves: The Christ has brought to earth the non-earthly forces that can help us to develop aspects that the earth can never help us to develop. We must take hold, with the whole of our being, of what to begin with is more in form of concepts, of ideas. We must use this to help us recognize the Christ as the One who has come to redeem our humanity. We must come to recognize Him as the spirit who will make it possible that we do not need to stay united with the earthly realm, we might say; that we will not be buried on earth, as it were, for all eternity, with the potential of development beyond this earth remaining undeveloped. When we thus come to see Christ as the One who will redeem our essential human nature, when we are able to see the way this world is made and come to feel there must be something within this earthly realm that will take us beyond it, when we feel that it is He who will lead us to become complete human beings—then we feel the power of Christ within us. And we really must come to realize that we cannot seriously speak of progressive development to spirit-self, life-spirit and spirit-man unless we are aware that there is no point in speaking of these things unless we appeal to the Christ, for the Christ is the principle that can take our evolution beyond anything the earth is able to give.

Basically this is the most important issue at the present time. Many people today, particularly those in the civilized world, want to shape things in a certain way on this earth; they want the whole potential of human beings to be achieved by creating some particular social configuration or other in this earthly life. That, however, can never happen. We shall never be able to evolve a political or economic life of that kind, nor indeed a cultural life of that kind, that would be entirely of this earth and make us into complete human beings. People still believe that such things are possible at the present time. They are making attempts in that direction but fail to realize that there is something in us that can only be taken further by a principle from beyond the earth.

The Christ Jesus first appeared in a physical body at a time the essential nature of which I have already characterized from many different points of view. We are now living in an age where He is to appear again to human beings and in a form that I also spoke of on the last occasion. It is clealy impossible for us to go exhaustively into the renewal of the Mystery of Golgotha, but I want to refer to it again and from a particular point of view.

The scientific element and everything connected with it has grown particularly strong over recent centuries, from the beginning of the fifth post-Atlantean epoch. In a recent public lecture I called it the 'science-orientated spirit of the West'.[70] This science-orientated spirit of the West did not initially relate at all to the Christ spirit. If you take an honest, unbiased look at modern science you will find that it has no real relationship to the Christ spirit. The best demonstration of this is the following: As I have said before, Christianity first entered into Earth evolution at a time when remnants of ancient clairvoyance were still persisting, and people grasped it with those remnants of ancient clairvoyance. Christianity then continued as a tradition. It gradually came to be diluted more and more to mental concepts, but it survived as a tradition. Finally it became mere word wisdom, but nevertheless it survived as a tradition. Over the last three or four centuries, however, the scientific spirit appeared on the scene. It also addressed itself to the Gospels. Very many people did and indeed still do today revere the Gospels because they tell the secrets of Golgotha. The science-orientated spirit of the modern age however addressed itself to the Gospels—this was particularly in the 19th century—and found them to contain contradiction upon contradiction. Unable to comprehend, it interpreted the Gospels in its own way. Basically the situation is now that thanks to scientific penetration, the Christ element in the Gospels has dissolved, particularly in the theology of the most recent kind. It is no longer there. If modern theologians say that the Gospels tell us something or other about the Christ they are not being entirely honest, not entirely truthful, or they construe all kinds of conflicting ideas. So we may indeed say that modern scientific thinking has destroyed the spirit of Christianity that consisted of remnants of ancient clairvoyance, and persisted as a tradition based on those remnants of ancient clairvoyance. The reason is that initially the Christ spirit was not present in modern scientific thinking. Science will only be filled with the Christ spirit again when new life comes into it through vision; through the things modern spiritual science is seeking to achieve.

Modern spiritual science wants to be as scientific in its thinking as any other science. The aim is however not to have a dead science but to let it become inner experience, just as we have inner experience of the vital powers we have as human beings. This newly enlivened science will succeed in penetrating to the Christ again.

What form will this enlivened science take? Some things are in preparation now, but I regret to say that they have not attracted much interest. I think I ought to mention that in the early nineties—well, in fact in the late eighties—of the last century I drew attention to a certain connection which exists between the way Schiller developed and the way Goethe developed.[78] I spoke of Schiller's attempt to solve the ridddle of human evolution in his own way, in his letters on aesthetic education. He started with completely abstract ideas. The first was the idea of logical necessity. He said to himself: 'This logical necessity is compulsive for us human beings. We have to think lilogically. Freedom does not exist when logic has to be used to analyze something, for we are then subject to the laws of logic. Freedom does not exist in that case.' The second idea in Schiller's mind was that human beings have natural needs; this concept encompasses everything that is instinctive and arises from the human capacity to have sensual desires. In this respect, too, human beings are not free but subject to necessity. In a certain way, therefore, human beings are the slaves of the highest intellectual achievement they are capable of, the logical necessity their abstract intellect is able to perceive by the process of reasoning. On the other hand, natural needs, human instincts, also rule and enslave human beings. It is possible, however, to find a middle position between logical thinking and instinctive feelings. Schiller felt that this middle state came to realization above all in the work of creative artists and in aesthetic pleasures. When we look at something beautiful or create something beautiful we are not thinking logically, yet our thoughts are at a spiritual level. We link ideas, but in doing so we do not pursue the logical connection but rather consider aesthetic appearance. On the other hand art seeks to make everything it brings to revelation visual, apparent to the senses. The object of natural necessity, of our instincts are also visual and apparent to the senses. Schiller therefore concluded that art and aesthetic pleasures are on the one hand suppressing logic to some extent, so that it can no longer enslave us but in a way merges into the things over which we gain personal mastery, overcoming them. On the other hand art raises the instinctive element to the sphere of the spirit, or in other words art enables us to feel that the instinctive element is also spiritual. It enables us to make logic the object of personal experience. Schiller wanted to make this condition generally applicable to human beings, saying that when they were in this condition human beings were not enslaved by a higher principle, nor by a lower one, but were indeed free. He wanted it to be the power that also ruled society—social life where people met face to face. People would then find that good things were also pleasing and that they could follow their instincts because they had purified them and made them spiritual, so that they could no longer drag them down. Human beings would then also share a social life that would give rise to a free social society. Schiller therefore considered three human conditions, albeit in an abstract way: the condition of ordinary physical needs, the condition of logical necessity, and the free condition of aesthetic experience.

Schiller developed this view of life in the early 1890s. He put it all into his letters on aesthetic education which he then presented to Goethe. Goethe was quite a different type of human being from Schiller. He felt: 'This man Schiller is trying to solve a certain riddle, the riddle of the essential human nature, of human evolution and human freedom.' Goethe was a more complex and profound character, however, and for him the issue could not be simply resolved by taking three abstractions and construing the whole essence of human evolution from them. Instead, the 'tale' of the green Snake and the beautiful Lily shone forth in his mind. Something like twenty different figures represented the potential capacities of the human soul, and the relations between them reflected human evolution. Schiller attempted to build everything up on the basis of three abstract ideas. Goethe's way was to create a picture composed of twenty Imaginations. The two men understood each other in a way. What exactly was it that they had done? Schiller used a scientific approach in writing his letters on aesthetic education. He really proceeded in exactly the scientific spirit that later became the scientific spirit of the 19th century. He did not go as far as that 19th century scientific spirit, however. He still remained at a personal level, as it were. 19th century science completely excluded the personal aspect and took pride in being entirely impersonal. The more impersonal knowledge can be made, the closer scientists feel they are to this ideal. 19th century scientists said, and present-day scientists still say: 'We know this and we know that about one thing or another. We know it in a way that is the same for every individual, so that there is no personal element in it.' Knowledge excludes the personal element to such an extent that modern people are only satisfied with their science once it has been coffined in the tombs we must come to recognize as the 'giant's tombs' of the life of the mind and spirit of today, i.e. in libraries, those tombs of the modern mind and spirit. Dead knowledge is stored in libraries, and we go there when we need some bone or other that we want to include in a dissertation or in a book. Those tombs are the true ideals of the modern scientific spirit. People walk about among all the highly objective knowledge stored there, but their personal interest is somewhere else; it is definitely not in there.

Schiller did not go as far as that in his letters on aesthetic education. He stayed at the personal level. He wanted personal enthusiasm, personal engagement, for every idea he developed. This is important. His letters on aesthetic education are certainly abstract, yet there is still the breath of an individual spirit in them. Knowledge was still felt to be connected with one's personal individuality. Schiller's abstract ideas therefore still had a personal element in them. He did not yet allow ideas to leave that realm and enter into a totally objective and impersonal, inhuman sphere. He did however go as far as the development of abstract ideas. Goethe did not find it possible to form such abstract ideas. He continued to use images, but he was very careful about this. He lived in an age when spiritual science could not yet be established. He felt some hesitation about sharply defining the images he presented in his 'tale' of the green Snake and the beautiful Lily. He was hinting that he was really concerned with a social life of the future. This comes clearly to expression in the conclusion of the 'tale' of the green snake and the beautiful Lily. Goethe did not want to go as far as hard and fast definitions. He did not say that social life should have three aspects, like the three aspects represented by the Golden King as the king of wisdom, the Silver King as the king of outward show—of a life setter please note omission of semblance, political life—and the Brazen king who might represent life in the material sphere, in the economic sphere. Goethe also represented the centralized state in the figure of the King of Mixed Metals who collapsed in a heap. He did not, however, get to the point of making sharp definitions. It was not a time when such delicate fairy-tale figures could be converted into solid characterizations of social life. I think you will agree that Goethe's figures were subtle fairy-tale figures. The time had not yet come when ideas that were still half fantasy and half living in Imaginations could be applied to outer life.

Years ago the idea came up of putting on a play in Munich and the intention was to present the creative potential of the essential values to be found in Goethe's 'tale' of the green snake and the beautiful Lily on the stage. This proved impossible. The whole thing had to be made much more real. The outcome was the mystery play *The Portal of Initiation*. It is more than obvious that in Goethe's day the time had not yet come when things which had to be presented in subtle fairy-tale images could be transformed into the real characters that appear in *The Portal of Initiation*. When *The Portal of Initiation* was being written the time had indeed come when one would soon be able to carry these things out into life. It was not enough, therefore, merely to interpret the Golden King, the Silver King, the Brazen King and the King of Mixed Metals. It had to be shown that the social life of today, where the centralized state is supposed to encompass everything, must smash itself to pieces, and that clear distinction must be made between the life of mind and spirit (Golden King), the political element (Silver King) and the economic aspect (Brazen King). My book *Towards Social Renewal* is Goetheanistic, if properly understood, but it represents the Goetheanism of the 20th century.

What I am saying is that Goethe and Schiller were able to reach a certain point in their day and age, Schiller in developing abstract ideas in his letters on aesthetic education, and Goethe in his images.

Goethe could get pretty nasty when other people tried to interpret his images. He had the feeling that the time had not yet come to transform these images into concrete forms that would apply to life. This shows very clearly that Schiller's and Goethe's time was not the time when the modern scientific spirit could be allowed to become inhuman and objective; it still had to be kept at a personal level. We will have to return to that level, and we can only do so with the help of spiritual science. Spiritual science must guide us to find the reality of what Schiller attempted to express in abstract ideas in his letters on aesthetic education and what Goethe, trying to solve the same riddle, hinted at in his 'tale' of the green Snake and the beautiful Lily.

The scientific spirit has to become personal again. The earth cannot help us with this. Science itself has to become Christ filled. By bringing the Christ idea into science we create the first beginnings for an evolution of the spirit-self.

Let us be clear about this: The earth has encouraged us to develop the ego. In its decline it will still be encouraging us to develop the ego yet further. This earth is something we shall have to leave behind in order to continue evolution on Jupiter and so on. We cannot connect the concept of ourselves as complete human beings with this earth. We have to take our human beingness back from the earth, as it were. If we were to develop only the earth-related science towards which Schiller and Goethe did not want to go—Schiller by keeping his abstract ideas personal, Goethe by not going beyond half-developed Imaginations—if we were to take our cues only fron the ingredients of the earth, we could never develop the spirit-self. All we could develop would be a dead science. We would therefore be adding more and more to the field strewn with corpses to be found in our libraries, in our books, where everything human is excluded. We would walk about among these 'thought-corpses', they would cast their spell upon us, and we would thus live up to Ahriman's ideal. One of the things Ahriman wants for us is that we produce lots of libraries, storing lots of dead knowledge all around us. The ancient Egyptians walked among their tombs, even the early Christians walked about among dead bodies, and Ahriman wants us to do the same. He wants human nature to slide back more and more into mere instinct, into egotistical instincts, and he wants all the thoughts we are able to muster to be stored in libraries. It is possible to imagine that a time will come when a young gentleman or even a young lady, aged somewhere around twenty or twenty-three, cannot think of a way of progressing in the world of the Silver King— in external terms we call that taking one's doctor's degree. Little rises from below in the human being; if one wanted to write a doctorate thesis on what arises out of one's human nature—I am of course assuming that a time may come when Ahriman has won the day!—such a thesis would be rejected as being subjective and personal. The young person would therefore visit libraries, taking up one book after another and probably basing his or her choice on catalogues listing all references to one particular key word. A new key word would mean taking out yet another book. The whole thing would then be put together to make a thesis. Only the outer physical individual would actually be involved in all this, however. The young man or woman would be sitting at a desk piled with books. Personal involvement would consist in getting hungry when one has been at it for a few hours, and this hunger would be felt to be something that effects one personally. Personal involvement might also come in because one had human relationships with certain commitments that would have to be met when they came to mind after those few hours. The books would then be shut and all personal conncetion with them would cease. The thesis made up from what one has found in various books would then be yet another book, a small one or a large tome; it would go to join the others on the library shelves and wait for someone to come and use it. I am not sure if this stage has already been reached somewhere today, but if Ahriman's ideal ever comes to realization that is exactly how it will be. It would be a terrible situation. Human individuality would wither away in such a terrible objective, non-human and impersonal situation.

To combat this, knowledge has to become a personal matter. Libraries should shrink if possible, and people should carry the things that are written in books in their souls. Spirit-self can only develop out of knowledge made personal, and that cannot happen unless people learn about the things that are not of this earth. The earth has passed the mid-point of its evolution. It is dying. Knowledge is dying in our libraries. It is also dying in our books, for they are the coffins of knowledge. We must take this element of knowledge back into our individuality. We must carry it in us. Help will come above all from the renewal of the Mystery of Golgotha. This will help people who have knowledge; it will help the followers of the Golden King.

New life must also come in another sphere, the sphere of rights. Human beings have as little personal connection with the legal system nowadays as they have with the sphere of knowledge. I have presented a small but definite proof of this in a recent public lecture.[79] I said that the German Empire had free and equal general suffrage. You could not have asked for anything better. But did those voting rights relate to life? Did people cast their votes in a way that was in accord with this franchise? Was there something alive in the configuration of the German Empire that arose because of this franchise? Absolutely not. The franchise was merely written in the Constitution. It was not alive in people's hearts. A time must come when people will no longer need to lay down as an objective Constitution how one human being should relate to another; then living relationships between people will give rise to law that is also alive. What need is there for written constitutions when people have the right feeling for their relationship as one human being to another and when this relationship comes to be a personal matter? In the last three decades of the 19th century human relations grew impersonal, and they have remained impersonal under the strong materialism of the 20th century. The law will only come alive when human beings have the Christ spirit within them.

In the sphere of rights, then, people must become followers of the Silver King. In economic life, on the other hand, they must become followers of the Brazen King. This means no more and no less than that the abstract ideal of brotherhood or companionship must become something real. How can companionship become real? By associating, by truly uniting with the other person, by no longer fighting people with different interests but instead combining those different interests. Associations are the living embodiment of companionship. The life-spirit must be alive in the sphere of rights, and with the Christ spirit brought into economic life, spirit-man will come to life in its first beginnings through associations. The earth, however, yields none of this. Human beings will only come to this if they let the Christ, who is now approaching in the ether, enter into their hearts and minds and souls.

You see, therefore, that the spiritual renewal of the Mystery of Golgotha, as we might call it, relates to what anthroposophical cosmology teaches. We come to see this when we are able to say to ourselves that we have the potential to develop spirit-self, life-spirit and spirit-man. Our thinking has grown so abstract, however, that is seems terribly dry and prosaic to hear that something as sublime and spiritual as the spirit-man, must first of all show itself in associations formed in economic life—in that 'low' economic life which has to do with material things. Surely a spiritual scientist cannot refer to economic life without 'lowering' himself? A spiritual scientist has to unite people in conventicles where no one speaks of anything connected with food and drink and one lives entirely in 'the spirit', which in fact means in abstract ideas.

The fact is however that when these people have been sitting in their conventicles or sects for long enough and have found their inner gratification they will finally emerge and of course take bread and— well, let us say 'water' lest we really offend. As a rule terribly little of all the principles they have established to gratify their souls in those conventicles will find application in life outside.

The true life of the spirit exists only where it is strong enough to overcome material life—and not leave it to one side as something that enslaves and compels us. This is something you really must come to realize.

I think when we come to consider things like these we realize that we must be serious in our approach to present-day life. Yet this seriousness can only come to full realization if we enter into things as deeply as spiritual science enables us to do. You see, the spiritual can only be brought close to human individuals through spiritual science. In a way Schiller and Goethe were the last who could still keep to the personal level, and this was due to something still accessible to them from the past. Schiller did not allow abstract ideas to develop the icy coldness of modern ideas. Goethe kept his Imaginations at a personal level and did not let them break through entirely into outer life.

Today we must go beyond this point. In the rough and tumble of present-day reality we cannot do anything with aesthetic letters— except maybe at aesthetic tea parties—nor with 'fairy-tales'. At most one might perhaps have beautiful conversations about them in the salons; even in those caricatures of salons that have now become lecture theatres for modern literature and are competing with the old-established professorial chairs. What is needed today is that we break through into life with the things that Goethe and Schiller still kept at the personal level. This will need powerful ideas and on the other hand also powerful Imaginations; a true spiritual understanding of the outer world must arise. To achieve this, we must fill ourselves with the Christ spirit. We will all need to believe in the Christ spirit in its true sense, believe that the Christ principle is something we have to unite with the part in us, as human beings, that will take us beyond this and make us into complete human beings by helping us to develop spirit-self, life-spirit and spirit-man.

All the things we encounter through spiritual science have an inner connection. Seeing through these inner connections we shall be able to see spiritual science in the right light and know that it belongs to the present age. We shall also know that in the present age spiritual science must be made to have a very real influence in all spheres of practical life.

This means, however, that spiritual science must take the whole of life extremely seriously. A true spiritual scientist would feel that it is inner frivolity to fail to be extremely serious, to fail to do more than fashion beautiful abstract ideas that are gratifying to the soul but are in no way able to break through into life.

This is something which has been weighing heavily on spiritual science for more than a year; it has been weighing heavily on those of us who are working here in Stuttgart. This work at Stuttgart has now made it our responsibility to bring spiritual science to bear in the practical life that immediately surrounds us on all sides. Principles that Goethe presented in fairy-tale images of a Golden, a Silver and a Brazen King, and a King of Mixed Metals who collapsed in a heap, must now be brought to bear in life and must become the threefold social order. You will remember that the King of Mixed Metals collapsed in a heap in the tale and certain persons came and licked up all the gold. If you take a good look at the world around us today you will see this phenomenon. In November 1918 Central Europe's King of Mixed Metals collapsed, and don't you see now how the various ministers who have held office since that time, the various leaders, are licking away and will go on licking until they have removed all the gold? Then the whole form of the Mixed King, a form empty of all spirit, will collapse, and people will be horrified. So we really ought to be serious—not about fairy-tale images of a Golden, a Silver, and a Brazen King, but with firm understanding for the three elements of the social organism: the cultural and spiritual element, the element of the political sphere, i.e. the state, and the economic element.

It has to be said, however, that when one comes to speak of these things two thoughts immediately come to mind. One of these I want to talk about today, for the longer we have to go on working like this in Stuttgart the more obvious it becomes that, for the time being at least, it is simply impossible to find time to talk to the friends who have got used to coming and asking my advice in earlier years. For a long time now I have had to put people off, when they wanted to discuss things that it certainly has previously been possible to discuss in private, promising to try again later on. Although my visits have been getting longer and longer, all efforts have had to be concentrated on the great task. I feel it really has to be said that, this time in particular, it has been quite impossible to consider personal requests. This is as painful for me as it is for you and I know that we cannot go on like this in the long run, for that would deprive the Anthroposophical Movement of its foundations. We would be building on shifting grounds in that case.

On the other hand it also has to be realized that people always like to cling to the old ways. Yet we are doing something entirely new in really getting to grips with the Golden, the Silver and the Brazen King, as I would like to call it. It is an extremely serious matter. Spiritual science cannot do such a thing as licking the gold away from the King of Mixed Metals who is collapsing in a heap, and some people take this amiss. I know I am poking around in a hornets' nest, but I shall have to poke around in quite a few hornets' nests, for example by characterizing a person such as Hermann Keyserling [80] who is simply not telling the truth and is a liar.

Some people say there is too much criticism within the Anthroposophical Movement today. But let me repeat once again what

I have said many times before: These people see what we have to do in order to defend ourselves—and they take exception to this. Exception is even taken by people who are sitting in this room and listening to the things that are being said. And they never say a word to give the lie to the people who throw mud at us from the outside—for that would mean becoming argumentative oneself. It is considered unkind for an anthroposophist to call someone a liar, when that is in fact the truth. Yet anyone who wants to tell lies about the Anthroposophical Movement is allowed to fling any kind of lie at us. The journal of our movement for a threefold order is often considered too polemical. You should turn against those whom we are simply forced to argue against; you should have the courage to address your words to them and not to us, for we are simply forced to defend ourselves. But that is a familiar bad habit. It shows that people are more interested in an Anthroposophy that provides self-gratification and not in a serious Anthroposophy that is considering the great problems of the present age.

Now and then it is really necessary to speak very seriously about these things. The things I said with reference to Count Keyserling in my public lecture, for instance, relate not only to the things said about Anthroposophy in that quarter; they relate to the whole inner insincerity of that kind of intellectual life. Read the chapter entitled 'What we need. What I want' in his most recent book.[81] It does not say anything about Anthroposophy, but you will find there the whole schematism of unsubstantial ideas that is wholly without content; yet you get stuffed shirts who will say that they get such a lot out of it. That of course is the great evil in our time, that people reject the things that take their substance from the spirit—the living spirit—and want only to have the empty words, mere shells of words.

If people go on wanting things like this they will destroy humanity. The hollow phrases coming from that source—even if they are called the *Diary of a Philosopher*[82]—undermine the whole of human culture. What are they, these hollow phrases? They are the phrases one produces if one licks the King of Mixed Metals. You may be fairly brutal in your licking, like some of the socialist leaders today, or you may be wearing elegant patent-leather boots like Count Keyserling—it really makes no difference.

I may be putting these things sharply, but please do not think this reflects an emotional involvement. They are put sharply because it has to be said, unfortunately, that there are some who want to be counted among the anthroposophists but whose hearts are not really in it. They cannot be sufficiently serious, they do not want to be sufficiently serious, they do not want their hearts to be involved. It is not being unkind to speak the truth when it is necessary to do so. But let me ask you if it is kind of anyone, who wants to be one of us, to allow others to sling mud at us and then call us unkind when we have to defend ourselves? It may seem regrettable that we have to use sharp words to defend ourselves, but just because of this you ought to uphold those sharp words and not indulge in feelings and the like and somehow or other start repeating the rubbish literary hacks have been producing—saying that polemics are not justifiable and are unkind.

The difficulty is that within the movement that is to develop as the Anthroposophical Movement we find so few people who are wholeheartedly with us. When it is necessary to achieve the kind of thing that we are supposed to achieve through the Anthroposophical Movement we need many such individuals today. We have found dedicated people in many different fields, above all the Waldorf School teachers in the educational field. We have also found dedicated individuals in some other fields—but it is simply not enough. The number of those who simply do not want to become completely involved is extremely large, right here in our own ranks, and yet we need people to be fully dedicated to our cause. That is why we are making so little progress. As time went on we found again and again that when we really got down to it, many of the people who had put their names down so that they would be able to hear the things that are said within the movement were in a way embarrassed to declare themselves openly for us on the outside. We have heard it said again and again that it would be better not to use the name Anthroposophy in public; that one should leave the name out and 'slip things in here and there' with reference to Anthroposophy. That is the delightful way people who do not want to take Anthroposophy seriously like to put it. So the gentleman, or particularly the lady, intends to 'slip something in' here and there by way of Anthroposophy, because she or he feels ashamed to speak openly about Anthroposophy. So they 'slip things in'! You won't have to be all that valiant, then, and you won't create any awkwardness—just 'let it slip in'.

Now is not the time to let things slip in, however. It is time to be open and honest and to use words that tell the truth about things. The people who are against us do not let things slip in, they put things bluntly. And it should be considered an outrage by all who have joined our ranks that someone like Count Keyserling has the cheek to say that this spiritual science of ours is materializing the life of the spirit, that it is a physical science of the spirit. We know that this man used sneaky ways to get hold of our lecture courses from a large number of people, in order to find out what is said in them, and all one can say is that in writing the things he is writing today he is quite deliberately writing untruths. We call it lying. Anyone who objects to our saying this is a lover of lies. Anyone who says that we are too argumentative when we are rightly speaking the truth has no feeling for the truth and is a lover of lies. The love of lies should not be our business in the Anthroposophical Movement, for we must love the truth. You must feel the whole weight of these words: to love the truth; not to love lies for the sake of convention, for the sake of a pleasant social life. To be easygoing when it comes to lies is just as bad as loving them. In the immediate future the world will not progress through frivolous indifference where lies are concerned, but only if we freely and openly profess ourselves for the truth. Anthroposophy has to consider serious and sublime spiritual matters, and we have never failed in this. Anyone who says that it is spiritual materialism to speak of Saturn, Sun and Moon when he is free to open my *Occult Science* and read what it says about Saturn, Sun and Moon, is indeed lying. It does not say anything about making the spirit into something material. People cannot be aware of the true seriousness of the situation if they ask that we use polite untruthful terms to address mud-slinging opponents.

These are the very things that reflect real love. Real love demands enthusiasm for the truth. The world will only progress if we show enthusiasm for the truth.

There are profound spiritual reasons why I have to say these things today, as I am about to leave you again for a while. I am very sorry that I am quite unable to talk to individuals at present, because there simply is not the time. Yesterday the friends of our movement for a threefold order and of the *Kommende Tag*[39] were again in session until 3 o'clock in the morning, and that is how it goes on, more or less day after day. I regret that many things have to be left aside, things that people have come to love. On the other hand there may be hope after all that, in view of the efforts now being made on a large scale, the Anthroposophical Movement will gain the rightful place in this world that it must gain, because it has the strength and the will to use the truth to move ahead. If we are to work in the truth, then we can do no other today than show untruthfulness up in its true light when it gets as blatant as this.

It has been necessary to remind you of our commitment to the truth. It is most necessary for all of us, dear friends, to let this spirit of longing for the truth fill our hearts and souls and minds. If it is still within the bounds of human capabilities, then this spirit in which we long for the truth will be the only thing that can prevent the barbarism that otherwise must come upon the human race. It will be the only spirit in which we shall make progress in a new culture which will be of the spirit.

Notes

This volume contains the stenographic records of lectures Rudolf Steiner gave to members of the Anthroposophical Society in Stuttgart during a number of visits to that city in 1920.

Sources. The lectures were taken down by a number of stenographers whose names are not recorded. The original German text of the book was based on the full texts written out by the stenographers afterwards. These are kept in the archives of the Rudolf Steiner Nachlass-Verwaltung in Dornach.

The German title of the book was not given by Rudolf Steiner but by the editors.

Other works by Rudolf Steiner that are part of the German Collected Works (Gesamtausgabe GA) are referred to by their GA numbers in these notes.

Most of the notes are translations of the notes in the German edition. A few have been added by the translator. These are identifiable from the letters TN at the beginning. Published German and English titles are shown in italics. Translations of German titles have been given initial capitals as appropriate if published in English; initial capitals have not been used where titles have merely been translated to inform English-speaking readers as to their meaning.

1 Ludwig Andreas Feuerbach, German philosopher. Referring to Feuerbach's anthropomorphism, Rudolf Steiner repeatedly quoted from his book *Das Wesen des Christentums* (1841), e.g. in a lecture given in Dornach on 15 October 1921 (*Anthroposophie als Kosmosophie*, GA 207, English title *Cosmosophy*).

Ludwig Buechner, German physician and materialist philosopher.

2 'Die Weisheitslehren des Christentums in Lichte der Theosophie' (The wisdom taught in the Christian faith in the light of Theosophy),Colmar, 21 November 1905 (no written record in existence).

3 Details not known.

4 Paul Deussen, philosopher and Sanscrit scholar.

5 Richard von Garbe, Sancrit scholar.

6 Johann Gottlieb Fichte, German philosopher. *Die Bestimmung des Menschen* 1800.

Friedrich Wilhem Joseph von Schelling German philosopher. *Bruno, oder über das göttliche and natürliche Prinzip der Dinge. Ein Gespräch* (Bruno, or concerning the divine and natural principle of things. A dialogue).

Johann Christoph Friedrich von Schiller, German dramatist, poet and historian.

Briefe über die ästhetische Erziehung des Menschen (letters on aesthetic education) 1795.

7 Ralph Waldo Trine, American writer.

8 Stuttgart, 21 December 1919. In *Weltsilvester and Neujahrsgedanken* GA 195. English in *The Cosmic New Year*. London: Rudolf Steiner Publishing Co. 1938.

9 A. Ferrière, La loi du progrès économique et la justice sociale. *Suisse-Belgique Outremer* juillet-aout 1919; **1**:no.3-4

10 Grigoriy Efimovich Rasputin, reputed 'holy man' who influenced the Tsarina and Tsar Nicholas II of Russia.

TN. William II (1859-1941), third German emperor and ninth king of Prussia.

11 Dr Roman Boos, anthroposophical lecturer, writer in the field of social sciences. Pioneer of the Threefold Movement.

12 TN. *plaisanterie*—joke; *méchanceté*—spitefulness, malice.

13 Prince-Archbishop Johann Baptist Katschthaler, Salzburg, Austria. Pastoral of 2 February 1905 entitled 'Die dem katholischen Priester gebührende Ehre' (The honour due to Catholic priests), reprinted in Carl Mirbt *Quellen zur Geschichte des Pabsttums and des römischen Katholizismus* (Sources relating to the history of the papacy and of Roman Catholicism) 5. Aufl. Tübingen 1934, S. 497 ff. The passage relating to the powers of consecration is given below.

'Honour your priests, for they have the power of consecration. Catholic priests have this wonderful power of consecration, Protestant pastors do not. This power of consecration, to make the Body of the Lord be present, with the precious Blood, with the whole of His sacred humanity and His divine nature in the Bread and the Wine—that is a great and sublime power, a truly extraordinary power! Where in heaven is a power like that of the Catholic priest to be found? Among the angels? Or does the Mother of God have it? Mary conceived Christ, the Son of God, in her womb and gave birth to Him in the stable in Bethlehem. Yes. But consider what happens during Holy Mass! Does not the same thing happen, as it were, when the priest raises his hands in blessing during the consecration? Christ is really and truly made to be present, to be reborn, as it were, in the Bread and the Wine. Mary bore her child in Bethlehem, wrapping it in swaddling clothes; a priest does the same, as it were, placing the wafer on the corporal cloth. *Mary brought her child into the world just once.* But see, *a priest does this not once, but many hundreds and thousands of times, each time he celebrates the Mass. There, in the stable, the child* which Mary gave to the world *was small, capable of suffering and mortal.* Here, on the altar, *in the hands of the priest, we have Christ in His glory, not capable of suffering and also immortal*, sitting in heaven to the right of the Father, glorious and triumphant, perfect in every regard. Do priests merely make the Body and Blood be present? No. They *sacrifice*, offering sacrifice to the Heavenly Father.

This is the same sacrifice that Christ brought by shedding His blood on Calvary and bloodlessly at the Last Supper. There the eternal High Priest Jesus Christ sacrificed His Flesh, His Blood and His very Life to the Heavenly Father; here, at the Mass, He does the same through his representative, the Catholic priest. He ordained priests to take His place so that they might continue the same sacrifice that He had brought. He has transferred to them the authority over His sacred humanity, giving them power over His body, as it were. A Catholic priest is able not only to make Him be present on the altar, lock Him up in the tabernacle, take Him out again and give Him to the faithful to eat, he is actually able to offer Him, the Son of God become Man, as a bloodless sacrifice for the living and the dead. Christ, the only begotten Son of the Father by whom heaven and earth were created and who sustains the whole world, submits to the Catholic priests in this respect.'
(*Italics as in the original text given by Mirbt.*)

14 '*Suprema lex regis voluntas*'. William II (see note 10) wrote this in the Golden Book of the City of Munich. See also J. von Kürenberg *War alles falsch? Das Leben Kaiser Wilhelms II.* (Was it all wrong? A life of the emperor William II. Translated into English and published in 1954, but exact English title not known), Basle-Olten 1940; German edition S. 190.

15 Dionysius the Areopagite (an Athenian converted by St Paul): 'On the Heavenly and Ecclesiastical Hierarchies' and The hierarchy of the church,' in *Die angeblichen Schriften des Areopagiten Dionysius, übersetzt und mit Abhandlungen begleitet von J.G.V. Engelhardt* (Writings ascribed to Dionyius the Areopagite, translated and provided with commentaries by J.G.V. Engelhardt), part 2, Sulzbach 1823.

16 Aurelius Augustinus, *De Civitate Dei*, libri XII.

Dante Alighieri, *De Monarchia*.

17 Wycliffe, John, English reformer.

Hus, or Huss, John, Bohemian reformer, burned when the Council of Constance condemned his and Wycliffe's writings.

18 TN. Luke 17:20-21. Rudolf Steiner was quoting from the Luther Bible, but saying 'gods' instead of 'God'.

19 Grim, Herman, *Fragmente* (vol. 1), Berlin & Stuttgart, S. 212: 'For the people of today [1891], it is no longer the Wars of Liberation fought against Napoleon I that are the last important historical event in their lifetime, but the Wars of Liberation fought against Austria and France in the 1860s and 1870s. We have been a nation where children had to be taught that they would never be permitted to act freely in influencing the destinies of their country. Today, however, Germans are compelled to act in this way. Fifty years ago it would have been unthinkable to make it part of education to tell children that they would one day be citizens of a great united German Empire and that their duties towards God, the Emperor and

their country would one day also consist in having to elect someone to represent them in a German Parliament, basing their choice on their personal judgement of the country's needs. Just to utter such things would have sounded like high treason and might have ruined the life of the person who uttered them.

20 'Der Weg zum gesunden Denken und die Lebenslage des Gegenwartsmenschen' (A way to develop sound thinking and people's life situation in the present day), Stuttgart 8 June 1920. Published in *Geisteswissenschaft und die Lebensforderungen der Gegenwart* No. 6, Dornach 1950. To be published in Germany in GA 355. No record of translation into English.

21 Lenin (formerly Ulyanov), Vladimir Ilyich, Russian revolutionary.

Trotsky, Leon (Lev Davidovich Bronstein), Russian revolutionary leader in 1917.

22 *Basler Vorwärts* of 2 June 1920. X.N., 'Die Politik der Sowjetregierung auf dem Gebiete der Religion' (Soviet government policies concerning religion).

23 See Franz Brentano, *Die Psychology des Aristoteles* (The psychology of Aristotle), Mainz 1867, S. 199 ff.

24 Traub, Friedrich, professor at Tuebingen University, author of *Rudolf Steiner als Philosoph und Theosoph* (Rudolf Steiner as a philosopher and theosophist), Tuebingen 1919.

25 For details relating to this see Boos, Roman, 'Aktenmäßige Darstellung der Hetze gegen das Goetheanum' (The virulent campaign againt the Goetheanum presented in documents), in *Rudolf Steiner/Roman Boos: Die Hetze gegen das Goetheanum* (The virulent campaign against the Goetheanum), Arlesheim 1920.

26 Refers to the Council's rejection of 'trichotomy'. Rudolf Steiner referred to this on a number of occasions, e.g. in *Bausteine zu einer Erkenntnis des Mysteriums von Golgatha* GA 175, 1st and 2nd lectures. English translation in *Cosmic and Human Metamporphoses*. H. Collison ed. London: Anthroposophical Publishing Co. 1926.

27 Mathilde Reichardt, a lady who published a book on science and moral philosophy in the form of letters to Moleschott in 1856, is able to lay undoubted and unenviable claim to rank first among those who turn moral concepts upside down. It is the opinion of this lady that moral philosophy merely has to ask whether a human individual develops his or her inherent traits in a balanced way. Yet nature—so she says—expresses a different intent in every human individual. She therefore does not hesitate to state 'that when someone has an inherent tendency to cheat and to steal, such a person can only be an entirely moral person if he or she is a cheat or a thief'. 'Someone born to be a thief has also been born with the right to live out those inherent tendencies, developing them to the full, for that is the only way in which he or she can be a strong and moral individual. And what applies

to thieves also applies to all other vices, including those born to be murderers.' (Quoted from Jürgen Bona Meyer, *Philosophische Zeitfragen*, Bonn 1874, S. 323 f.)

28 Vogt, Carl, champion of Darwinism.

Moleschott, Jakob, physiologist.

Buechner, Ludwig, German physician and materialist philosopher.

29 *Die Philosophie der Freiheit* (1894), GA. 4. English: *The Philosophy of Freedom*. M. Wilson tr. London: Rudolf Steiner Press 1970.

30 'Die Erziehung und der Unterricht gegenüber der Weltlage der Gegenwart' (Education and teaching in the light of the present world situation), Stuttgart 10 June 1920. Published in *Geisteswissenschaft und die Lebensforderungen der Gegenwart* 6, Dornach 1950. To be published in GA 335. No record of translation into English.

31 *Die Kernpunkte der Sozialen Frage in den Lebensnotwendigkeiten der Gegenwart und Zukunft* (1919) GA 23. English translation: *Towards Social Renewal*. F.T. Smith tr. London: Rudolf Steiner Press 1977.

32 See Rudolf Steiner's *Mein Lebensgang* (1923-25) GA. 28. English translation: *Rudolf Steiner: An Autobiography*. R. Stebbing tr. New York: Rudolf Steiner Publications 1977.

33 *Von Seelenrätseln* (Riddles of the soul) (1917) GA. 21. Parts translated into English in *The Case for Anthroposophy*. Owen Barfield tr. London: Rudolf Steiner Press 1970.

34 Molt, Emil, see ref. 37.

Kühn, Hans, writer and publisher.

Unger, Carl, grad. engineer, owner of machine tool works, member of Council of the German Anthroposophical Society from 1905, lecturer and writer. Shot by a mentally sick individual in Nuremberg in 1929.

Leinhas, Emil, businessman, managing director of Der Kommende Tag AG (see ref. 39), writer.

35 Seiling, Max, first a follower then an opponent of Rudolf Steiner. Bore the title Privy Councillor.

TN. Rudolf Steiner used word-play here, calling *Hofrat* (Privy Councillor) Seiling an *Un-Rat*. The word *Unrat* means garbage, refuse, ordure.

36 *An das deutsche Volk und an die Kulturwelt!* (Appeal to the German nation and

the civilized world), pamphlet, 1919, reprinted a.o. in *Towards Social Renewal* (ref. 31).

37 Appeal to establish a Council for Culture. Whitsun 1919, signed by many well-known figures in cultural life.

38 Waldorf School: intergrated primary and secondary school established by Emil Molt in 1919 for the children of workers in the Waldorf Astoria Cigarette Factory and the general public. This was done under the guidance of Rudolf Steiner who also appointed the teachers and himself gave the preparatory teachers' seminars.

39 *Der Kommende Tag*, Aktiengesellschaft zur Förderung wirtschaftlicher and geistiger Werte (join-stock company for the promotion of economic and cultural values), established in Stuttgart in March 1920. Rudolf Steiner was Chairman of the Board until 1923. The company became a victim of post-war inflation in Germany and had to be dissolved in 1925.

40 Stuttgart 16 June 1920; published in *Landwirtschaft und Industrie/Neuordnung des Bodenrechtes als soziale Forderung der Gegenwart* (Agriculture and industry/New proposals for land ownership as a social requirement for the present age); quoted from the writings and lectures of Rudolf Steiner, Roman Boos ed., Stuttgart 1957, S. 84 ff. (to be published in GA 335). No record of translation into English.

41 Spengler, Oswald, German historic writer. *Der Untergang des Abendlandes (Decline of the West*, C.F. Atkinson tr.) Munich, vol. 1, 1918, vol. 2, 1922.

42 *Die Philosophie des Thomas von Aquino*. 3 lectures given in Dornach on 22-24 May 1920. GA 74. English translation: *The Redemption of Thinking*. A.P. Shepherd, M.R. Nicoll tr. London: Hodder & Stoughton 1956.

43 *Durch den Geist zur Wirklichkeits-Erkenntnis der Menschenrätsel*: Philosophie und Anthroposophie. Vier Märchen (aus den Mysteriendramen). Anthroposophischer Seelenkalender. Der Seelen Erwachen, 7. und 8. Bild. [Discovering the reality of the riddles of human nature through the spirit. Philosophy and Anthroposophy. Four tales (from the Mystery Plays). Calendar of the Soul. The Soul's Awakening, scenes 7 and 8]. Berlin 1918.

44 TN. Eckhart, Johannes, known as Meister Eckhart, German mystic.

45 *Wie erlangt man Erkenntnisse der höheren Welten?* 1904. GA 10. English translation: *Knowledge of the Higher Worlds*. G. Metaxa tr., D.S. Osmond, C. Davy rev. London: Rudolf Steiner Press 1976.

46 Trinity Group: a sculpture in wood generally referred to as the Group Sculpture at the Goetheanum in Dornach, Switzerland. It shows the Representative of Humanity between Lucifer and Ahriman.

47 Dessoir, Max. *Vom Jenseits der Seele. Die Geheimwissenschaften in kritischer Betrachtung* (From the beyond of the soul. A critical assessment of the occult sciences). S. 254 ff. Stuttgart 1917.

48 *Die geistige Führung des Menschen und der Menschheit*, 1910. GA 15. English translation: *The Spiritual Guidance of Man and Humanity*. H.B. Monges tr. New York: Anthroposophical Press 1970.

49 Prof. Hugo Fuchs, Goettingen. See also Rudolf Steiner, 'Ein paar Worte zum Fuchs-Angriff' (A few words on the attack made by Fuchs), in *Dreigliederung des sozialen Organismus* 2. Jahrg. Nr. 5 (Aug. 1920); reprinted in *Aufsätze zur Dreigliederung des sozialen Organismus und zur Zeitlage 1915-1921* GA 24.

50 *Dreigliederung des sozialen Organismus* 2. Jahrg. Nr. 4, Beilage (Juli 1920).

51 Atwood, George. English mathematician, invented a machine to illustrate the motion of a body falling under the action of gravity.

52 *Von Jesus zu Christus* GA 131. English translation: *From Jesus to Christ*. H. Collison tr., C. Davy rev. London: Rudolf Steiner Press 1973.

53 *Die Geheimwissenschaft im Umriß* 1910. GA 13. English translation: *Occult Science. An Outline*. G and M. Adams tr. London Rudolf Steiner Press 1969.

54 Wasmann, Erich, entomologist. Major researches on ants. The MS of the lecture is not quite clear at this point, and the German editors have added the words in [ ].

55 Literally Goethe said the following:
'It is said that the truth lies halfway between two contradictory opinions. Far from it! The problem lies in between, it cannot be beheld; life, for ever active, calmly thought' *Maximen und Reflexionen).*
The MS of the lecture had been quoted verbatim in the earlier German edition but has been found to be incomplete and therefore was revised for the German edition on which this translation is based.

56 Christlieb, Max, a friend from Rudolf Steiner's time at Weimar who had done much to make *The Philosophy of Freedom* more widely known when it had just been published. See also Rudolf Steiner and Christlieb Ludwig Kleeberg, *Wege und Worte*, 2. Aufl. 1961 S. 76 ff. This also refers to the Marburg occasion.

57 'Die großen Aufgaben von heute im Geistesleben, Rechtsleben und Wirtschaftsleben. Eine dritte Gegenwartsrede.' (Major presentday tasks in cultural life, the sphere of rights and in economic life. A third topical talk.) Publ. in Rudolf Steiner: *Drei Gegenwartsreden* (Three topical talks), Heft 8, Dornach 1952. To be published in GA 335.

58 See conclusions of lectures given on 11 and 17 January 1920 in *Geistige und soziale*

Wandlungen in der Menschheitsentwickelung. GA 196, S. 52 & 82 ff. (Cultural and social changes in the evolution of humanity). No record of translation into English.

59 Rohm, Karl, editor of the journal *Der Leuchtturm*, Lorch (Wuerttemberg).

60 Further details in E. Uehli, 'Die gestohlene Dreigliederung' in *Dreigliederung des sozialen Organismus* 2. Jahrg. Nr. 11 (Sept. 1920).

61 Knapp, Alfred, established 'Internationaler Orden für Ethik und Kultur' (International Order for Ethics and Culture).

62 Tagore, Sir Rabindranath, *Nationalism* (also translated into German).

63 James, William, American psychologist and pragmatic philosopher.

64 'Das Märchen von der grünen Schlange und der Lilie' (Tale of the green Snake and the Lily) in *Unterhaltungen deutscher Ausgewanderten* 1795, Weimarer Ausgabe, 18. Bd., S. 225 ff.

65 Humboldt, Karl Wilhelm von, *Ideen zu einen Versuch, die Grenzen der Wirksamkeit des Staates zu bestimmen* (Ideas for an attempt to determine the limits of effectiveness for a political state) 1792.

66 Wilson, Thomas Woodrow, *The State. Elements of Historic and Practical Politics* (also translated into German).

67 Keely, John Worrell. See also lecture given by Rudolf Steiner in Dornach on 1 Dec. 1918 in *Die soziale Grundforderung unserer Zeit/In geänderter Zeitlage* GA 186 S. 70 ff. English translation in *In the Changed Conditions of the Times*. O.D. Wannamaker tr. New York/London: Anthroposophic Press/Rudolf Steiner Publishing Co. 1941.

68 TN. The Franco-Prussian War 1870-71.

69 TN. Throughout this lecture Rudolf Steiner used an invented word, *Technizismen* (technicisms) for 'products of technology'.

70 Stuttgart 10 November 1920, 'Die Geisteskrisis der Gegenwart und die Kräfte zum Menschheitsforschritt' (The spiritual and cultural crisis of the present time and the forces that mean progress for humanity). To be published in GA 335.

71 Bayle, Pierre, French philosopher. Statement has not been traced to date.

72 Goethe, Johann Wolfgang von, *Die Leiden des jungen Werther* (The sorrows of Werther) 1775. Weimarer Ausgabe, 19. Bd.

73 Miller, Johann Martin. *Siegwart*, novel published in 1776 (2 years after *Werther*), very popular for a time.

74 Paquet, Alfons, writer. *Im kommunistischen Rußland In communist Russia) appeared in 1919.*

75 See also public lecture referred to in note 69.

76 Clemenceau, Georges. French physician and politician.

77 Harnack, Adolf von. German theologian.

78 'Goethe als Vater einer neuen Aesthetik' lecture to the Goethe Society in Vienna on 9 November 1888; first published in Vienna in 1889, reprinted in *Methodische Grundlagen der Anthroposophie 1884-1901* GA 30 and *Kunst und Kunsterkenntnis* GA 271. English translation: *Goethe as Founder of a New Science of Aesthetics.* G. Metaxa tr. Anthroposophical Publishing Co., 1922.

79 Stuttgart 16 November 1920, 'Die Wahrheit der Geisteswissenschaft und die praktischen Lebensforderungen der Gegenwart' (The truth of spiritual science and the practical requirements of present-day life). To be published in GA 335.

80 Keyserling, Hermann, Graf. German philosopher.

81 Keyserling, Hermann, *Philosophie als Kunst* (Philosophy as an art), Darmstadt 1920.

82 Keyserling, Hermann, *Das Reisetagebuch eines Philosophen* (*Travel Diary of a Philosopher*, 1925), Darmstadt 1919.

Index of Names

(R = passing reference)

Aquinas, St Thomas (1225-74)	74R
Aristotle (384-322 BC)	48
Arnet	51
Atwood, George (1746-1807)	88
Augustine, St (354-430)	33
Bayle, Pierre (1647-1706)	143, 144, 152R
Boos, Roman (1889-1952)	23, 52, 52
Buechner, Ludwig (1824-99)	6R, 54R, 97, 110R
Christlieb, Max (1862-1916) (not mentioned by name)	113R
Clemenceau, Georges (1841-1929)	151R
Dante Alighieri (1265-1321)	33R
Darwin, Charles (1809-82)	129
Dessoir, Max (1867-1947)	84R
Deußen, Paul (1845-1919)	18R
Dionysius the Areopagite	32R
Eckhart, Johannes (c. 1260-1327)	77, 88
Ferrière, Adolphe (1879-1960)	22R, 23R
Feuerbach, Ludwig (1804-72)	6
Fichte, Johann Gottlieb (1762-1814)	21, 22, 124
Fuchs, Hugo (not mentioned by name)	85
Garbe, Richard von (1857-1927)	18
Goethe, Johann Wolfgang von (1749-1832) (also Goetheanism)	21, 78, 111, 124 126, 127, 129, 130, 145, 159, 160, 161, 162, 163, 166
Grimm, Herman (1828-1901)	37R
Harnack, Adolf von (1851-1930)	151
Hegel, Georg Wilhelm Friedrich (1770-1831)	124, 129, 130
Herder, Johann Gottfried (1744-1803)	22, 124
Humboldt, Wilhelm von (1767-1835)	128R
Hus, Johann (c. 1369-1415)	34R
James, William (1842-1910)	125R
Katschthaler, Johann Baptist (1832-1914) (not mentioned by name)	31R, 53
Keely, John Worrell (1827-98)	132R, 133
Keyserling, Hermann (1880-1946)	168R, 169, 171

Knapp, Alfred	115R
Kuehn, Hans (1889-1977)	64R
Leinhas, Emil (1878-1967)	64R
Lenin, Vladimir Ilyich (1870-1924)	42R, 43, 60
Lessing, Gothold Ephraim (1729-81)	21
Marx, Karl (1818-83)	60
Metzdorff-Teschner, Elisabeth Mathilde	115R
Moleschott, Jakob (1822-93)	54R, 97, 110R
Molt, Emil (1876-1936)	64R
Nero, Lucius Domitius (37-68)	31
Paquet, Alfons (1881-1944)	149R
Plato (c. 427-c.347 BC)	48
Ranke, Leopold von (1795-1886)	12R
Rasputin, Grigoriy Efimovich (?1871-1916)	22R
Reichardt, Mathilde (not mentioned by name)	54
Rohm, Karl	114, 116
Schelling, Friedrich Wilhelm Joseph von (1775-1854)	21, 22, 124
Schiller, Johann Christoph Friedrich von (1759-1805)	22, 124, 126, 127, 128 159, 160, 161, 162, 163, 166
Seiling, Max (1852-1928)	64R
Spencer, Herbert (1820-1903)	129
Spengler, Oswald (1880-1936)	72R, 92, 93, 152
Tagore, Sir Rabindranath (1861-1941)	122R
Tauler, Johannes (c. 1300-61)	88
Tolstoy, Count Leo Nikolayevich (1828-1910)	133
Traub, Friedrich (b. 1860)	49, 51
Trine, Ralph Waldo (1866-1958)	22
Trotsky, Leon (1879-1940)	42R, 43, 60
Unger, Carl (1878-1929)	64R
Vogt, Carl (1817-1895)	54R, 97, 110R
Wasmann, Erich (1859-1931)	108R
William II (1859-1941)	22
Wilson, Thomas Woodrow (1856-1924)	128R, 151
Wycliffe, John (c. 1329-84)	34